Finnair

A Century of Nordic Aviation

JOZEF MOLS

KEY
Books

AIRLINES SERIES, VOLUME 5

Front cover image: The Airbus A350 XWB became the backbone of Finnair's Asian network. (Finnair)

Back cover image: Part of the Finnair fleet at Helsinki-Vantaa Airport. (Finnair)

Title page image: Finnair operates its Nordic and European network with a fleet of Embraer jets. (Finnair)

Contents page image: Aircraft tails at Helsinki-Vantaa Airport. (Finnair)

Published by Key Books
An imprint of Key Publishing Ltd
PO Box 100
Stamford
Lincs PE19 1XQ

www.keypublishing.com

The right of Jozef Mols to be identified as the author of this book has been asserted in accordance with the Copyright, Designs and Patents Act 1988 Sections 77 and 78.

Copyright © Jozef Mols, 2022

ISBN 978 1 80282 194 9

Typeset by SJmagic DESIGN SERVICES, India.

Contents

Introduction and Acknowledgements

When aviation historians dig into the history of European aviation, the names 'Junkers Flugzeugwerke AG' and 'Aero Oy' certainly catch the eye. These two companies are indeed the founders of the Finnish airline that would later become Finnair. Aero Oy was incorporated in 1923, with a 50 per cent participation from the German aircraft manufacturer. However, in 1925, Finnish investors bought back the German shares. With a small fleet of Junkers F 13 aircraft, Aero Oy started up services in Finland, Scandinavia and the Baltic states. The availability of transportation by air was more than welcome, as Finland is a big country with a rather small population, scattered in villages all over the country. In the beginning, Aero Oy had to operate seaplanes, as airports had yet to be constructed. When the number of passengers increased, Aero Oy also expanded its fleet to include Junkers G 24 and Junkers Ju 52 aircraft. With the outbreak of the war, Russian troops occupied Finland, later followed by German soldiers. Each time, Aero Oy's fleet was requisitioned by the Finnish Air Force, but the airline could, nevertheless, continue to operate a limited flight schedule.

After the war, the Finnish government took a participation in the airline, which then rapidly expanded with the purchase of Douglas C-47s, Douglas DC-2 and DC-3 aircraft, as well as de Havilland Dragon Rapides. The Convair 340 and 440 also joined the fleet. Therefore, one can say that Aero Oy really took flight after World War Two. Thanks to its geographical location, the airline – which was rebranded as Finnair – could start up routes to many destinations in the Soviet Union. With the introduction of jet aircraft, transatlantic flights were added. However, above all, Finnair expanded its network to the East. The airline became the first carrier to offer non-stop flights from Western Europe to Japan by flying directly north from Helsinki over the North Pole and back south through the Bering Sea. The transpolar route was shorter and, therefore, more comfortable for the passengers, and, as a result, the route would become one of Finnair's success stories. By using its geographic advantage, the airline continued to expand its network to the Far East. When China introduced its geopolitical plan to set up a new 'Silk Road', Finnair was well positioned in the Chinese market to benefit from this decision. Of course, the airline was also hit by economic crisis, the impact of major catastrophes in countries on its route network and COVID-19. However, while its management was trying to cope with the traffic restrictions, imposed as a result of the pandemic, it was, at the same time, taking steps to prepare Finnair for the post-pandemic period.

The story of Finnair is a very fascinating story and is worthwhile to be told. Although it is not possible to go into detail about all aspects of the carrier's history, I hope this book will – in a modest way – give an account of Finnair's activities, challenges and results. Therefore, I am very grateful to Key Publishing for the publication of this book, to all photographers who made pictures available that illustrate this book and to Finnair for allowing me access to their archives. And, of course, my thanks go to my partner, Marianne Van Leuvenhaege, for tolerating me spending so much time working on this publication and for proofreading the chapters of this book.

Jozef Mols
Wommelgem, 24 November 2021

Chapter 1

The Pre-War Years

The history of civil aviation in Finland actually begins in Estonia in 1918, when Bruno Lucander became involved as the general manager of Finland Spedition, a managerial group that ran the Finnish operations of the Estonian airline Aeronaut. In 1923, Aeronaut was acquired by the German company Junkers Flugzeugwerke AG, and German interests would dominate the Finnish aviation industry for years. At first, a Junkers F 13 was used on the route from Tallinn to Helsinki. The aircraft was a single-engine monoplane, equipped with a closed cabin and seats for four passengers. Aeronaut's use of it under Nordic conditions clearly proved that this aircraft was up to the challenge of operating under the demanding conditions of northern Europe, which made a deep impression on Lucander. Therefore, he made an agreement with Junkers to provide one F 13 and technical support in exchange for a 50 per cent participation in Aero Oy – a new airline in Finland. The company was entered into the trade register on 11 December 1923.[1] Besides Junkers, other shareholders included Bruno Lucander (who became the first chairman of the airline), Gustave Snellman and Fritiof Ahman. The first F 13 delivered to Aero Oy was registered in Germany (D-335), as the aircraft was too expensive to be bought and had to be leased. It arrived in Finland on 17 March 1924. Three days later, the aircraft made its first commercial flight by delivering 162kg of mail to the Estonian capital, Tallinn.[2] Hugo Junkers, who had designed the F 13, insisted that only pilots with a year's training on the type would be allowed to fly it. However, in the summer of 1924, Finnish pilot Gunnar Lihr started commercial flights with the aircraft after only one week of training on the type.

In the beginning, Aero operated from Katajanokka, near Helsinki, where, at that time, facilities consisted of a small terminal building and a seaplane ramp. The F 13 was equipped with floats during the summer, and in wintertime, skis allowed operations on snow and ice. This resulted in an interruption of traffic in spring and autumn when ice drifts prevented landing of seaplanes on the one hand, and the ice was not thick enough to allow ski-equipped planes to land on the other hand. By the end of the first year of operations, Aero purchased a second F 13, and on 2 June 1924, the airline started the Helsinki–Stockholm route (only during the summer) in competition with the newly founded Swedish company AB Aerotransport. As there was a good rail connection from Stockholm to Gothenburg, travellers were offered easy access to Copenhagen, Konigsberg and Berlin.[3] Aero also started flights to Turku and Vyborg in the same year, as well as to Riga. During its first year of operations, Aero Oy carried 534 passengers. In order to promote air travel, the airline offered 833 sight-seeing tours during 1925.

In 1925, Junkers amalgamated its Nord Europa Union and Trans Europa Union air transport subsidiaries into a single company, consisting of 16 airlines in nine countries. The new company, Europa Union, was then combined with another German airline – Aero Lloyd – to form Deutsche Lufthansa. Aero remained outside this group and support from Junkers diminished, as Junkers gave priority to its new German consortium. Aero Oy, therefore, turned to the government for financial assistance and obtained government-backed loans for the purchase of new aircraft. In 1926, the airline received this type of subsidy for the first time and took delivery of its first Junkers G-24. This three-engined aircraft was equipped with floats, but not with skis and, therefore, could only be operated in summertime. Aero remained reluctant to use land-based aircraft, as the Nordic countries, with their coastlines and lakes, were especially suited for seaplane traffic.

In 1927, Aero became a member of the International Air Traffic Association (IATA). A year later, the airline would receive considerable publicity in the international press when its F 13, flown by

Gunnar Lihr, took part in the search for the explorer Umberto Nobile's airship *Italia*, which had crashed near Spitsbergen. Lihr was able to rescue one of the expedition members. Two years later, the airline would receive even more press attention when the F 13 located the Norwegian vessel *Bratvaag*, which was carrying the remains of the crew of the ill-fated 1897 Andree Expedition from Spitzbergen.[4] By 1929, the year Chairman Lucander died, the Finnish investors in Aero Oy were able to buy back the remaining 50 per cent of shares previously held by Junkers. This way, Aero became an entirely Finnish-owned company. Nevertheless, Junkers would remain the company's major aircraft supplier in the early 1930s, providing five 14-passenger Junkers Ju 52s. Hugo Junkers did not fare well after the Nazis took power in Germany in 1933. He had to leave his own firm and he died in 1935. Subsequently, the company was nationalised. By that time, however, Aero had paid all its debts to Junkers, which had resulted from the purchase of new aircraft.

In the early 1930s, Aero Oy began to establish close relations with other Scandinavian airlines. The company started up nightly airmail services in cooperation with Swedish, Danish and Dutch airlines. However, while Aero Oy was still mainly operating seaplanes, land airports for passenger traffic had already been established in continental Europe to such an extent that creating air harbours for seaplanes in their expanding route networks was beginning to seem obsolete. As it was imperative to keep up with development, the planning of land airports around major cities in Finland started. In September 1935, Artukainen Field in Turku was the first land airport for passenger traffic in the country. It would become an important gateway for international traffic and an intermediate point on the route from Helsinki to the new Bromma airport near Stockholm. Construction of the Helsinki-Malmi Airport followed a few years later. Prior to its construction, the area of Tattarisuo was a worthless swamp. The selection of this site was a win-win situation for both the city of Helsinki and the Finnish government. The city would get rid of a piece of wasteland and the government could build the much-needed airport … at its own expense. However, the offer was turned down by the government and the city of Helsinki. In 1933, another location was found far away from Helsinki on the fields of Tuomarinkylä. This, however, was quality farmland and the farmers did not agree with this selection. So, finally, attention returned to the Tattarisuo location. An 800m runway was constructed, as well as a hangar, an administrative building with a passenger lounge, a restaurant, a meteorological station and a control tower. The airport terminal building was designed by Dag Englund, a well-known Finnish architect, and the airport as a whole became an impressive avant-garde achievement that won international recognition. The large hangar could accomodate up to six large Junkers Ju 52 aircraft and was fully equipped for maintenance and repairs. Operations began on 16 December 1936. AB Aerotransport operated its flight between Malmi–Turku and Stockholm. Aero Oy would join later when its Junkers Ju 52s were stripped of their floats and equipped with landing gear.[5] At that time, the airline halted its Katajanokka to Stockholm service operated by seaplanes. Passenger numbers had increased dramatically since the first Aero Oy flights. While the company had carried 534 passengers in 1924, by 1934, this number had increased to 6,550, 7,098 in 1935 and 8,702 in 1936.[6]

In order to extend its domestic network, Aero Oy took delivery of its first non-Junkers aircraft in 1937. The twin-engined de Havilland DH89A could transport seven passengers on scheduled domestic flights to Imatra, Tampere and Vaasa. As construction of airports in northern Finland went on, Aero Oy could extend its 'Arctic Air Express' on the route Helsinki–Tampere–Vaasa–Oulo–Kemi–Petsami, enabling travellers to fly from Helsinki to the Arctic Coast in one day. During the summer bathing season, a special service was also run between Stockholm and Mariehamm on the Aland Islands. The international network was extended as well. The Stockholm–Helsinki–Tallinn route was extended to Berlin via Riga and Kaunas. Additionally, services to Warsaw and Copenhagen were added. Due to this expansion, Aero Oy decided to order five more Junkers Ju 52s. With the Olympic Games planned for Helsinki in 1940, four Focke-Wulf Fw 200B Condor aircraft were ordered. These aircraft would not only increase the prestige of the Finnish carrier, but it would also enable its first intercontinental service to the US. The start of World War Two, however, curtailed Aero's plans. In 1939, war broke out across Europe. Russia invaded Finland on 30 November 1939 and Estonia a few weeks later. All available aircraft were requisitioned by the Suomen Ilmavoimat (Finnish Air Force) and would remain under military control until 1945. In the first months of the war, however, several requisitioned aircraft, flown by civilian pilots, would be used to evacuate Finnish children to Denmark.

Of course, Aero Oy was not the only airline that began operations in the pre-war years in Finland. The Karhumäki brothers were also interested in aviation. By the 1920s, they had already started to build aircraft of their own design. In 1929, they took up aerial photography (their company is still active in this field today). When, in 1932, the Finnish government started to make efforts to build up civil aviation, the Karhumäki brothers were issued a number of government contracts for regular mail delivery flights in parallel with Aero Oy. Some domestic passenger routes also were subsidised. Just like Aero Oy, the brothers used the government provided state-guaranteed loans to purchase a series of passenger planes. In 1936, they obtained six de Havilland DH89 Dragon Rapides, to service government mail contracts. Some of these aircraft were also used for aerial photography of frontier areas.

While Aero Oy was buying Junkers Ju 52s from Germany, and later DH89 Dragon Rapides, Veljekset Karhumäki took advantage of purchases by the Finnish Air Force. In its pre-war operations, the Ilmavoimat had bought a few Douglas DC-2 aircraft, but, finally, they decided to purchase up to 20 Douglas DC-3s as transport aircraft for the newly formed Para Jaeger unit. Some of these Dakotas were leased to Veljekset Karhumäki and others to Aero Oy. The leased aircraft were listed as Ilmavoimat reserve, and the civilian pilots who flew them became Ilmavoimat Reservists. When needed, the Ilmavoimat chartered back these aircraft from Veljekset Karhumäki, to use as paratrooper training aircraft.

The first aircraft of Aero Oy was registered in Germany. (Helsinki City Museum)

In wintertime, the Junkers aircraft used skis to operate on snow and ice. (Finnish Aviation Museum)

In summertime, the F 13s operated from water and were equipped with floats. (Helsinki City Museum)

Above: Arrival of a Junkers
F 13 in the winter of 1923.
(Helsinki City Museum)

Right: Departure of an
Aero Oy Junkers G 24.
(Finnair via Edvardsson)

Below: An Aero G 24 at its base
in 1934. (Helsinki City Museum)

ANTANUT
UTSTÄLLD AV
ISSUED BY
AERO O/Y

(Siinä tapauksessa, että yllämainittu yhtiö ei itse suorita kuljetusta, se toimii vain kuljetusyhtiön asioimistona.)
(Ifall ovannämnda bolag ej själv utför transporten betraktas det som det befordrande bolagets agentur.)
(In so far as the above-mentioned Company does not perform the carriage itself, it acts only as agent for the carrier.)

International Air Traffic Association'in jäsen
Medlem av International Air Traffic Association
Member of International Air Traffic Association
I. A. T. A

Kuljetusyhtiö on merkitty matkalippuun
Det fraktförande bolaget angives på biljetten.
The name of the carrier appears on the passenger ticket.

MENOLIPPU
TURBILJETT
SINGLE TICKET
No. OH 17874

SOTAVAARA EI SISÄLLY VAKUUTUKSEEN
KTS. KANNEN SISÄP.
FÖR KRIGSRISKER ANSVARAS EJ.
SE OMSLAGETS INSIDA.
NO LIABILITY FOR WAR RISKS.
SEE INSIDE OF COVER

Kuljetusmääräysten suhteen: katso takasivua.
Betr. transportbestämmelserna: se baksidan.
For conditions of carriage: see back.

Matkustajan nimi
Passagerarens namn
Passenger's name
LEHTELÄ

Oheellinen lippu on voimassa vain täydellisenä kansineen.
Medföljande biljett är giltig endast komplett inkl. pärmbladet.
The enclosed ticket is only valid when complete with cover.

Auton lähtöaika ja paikka
Avgångstid och plats för bussen till flygplatsen
Time and place of departure car service
klo 10⁰⁰ Aero

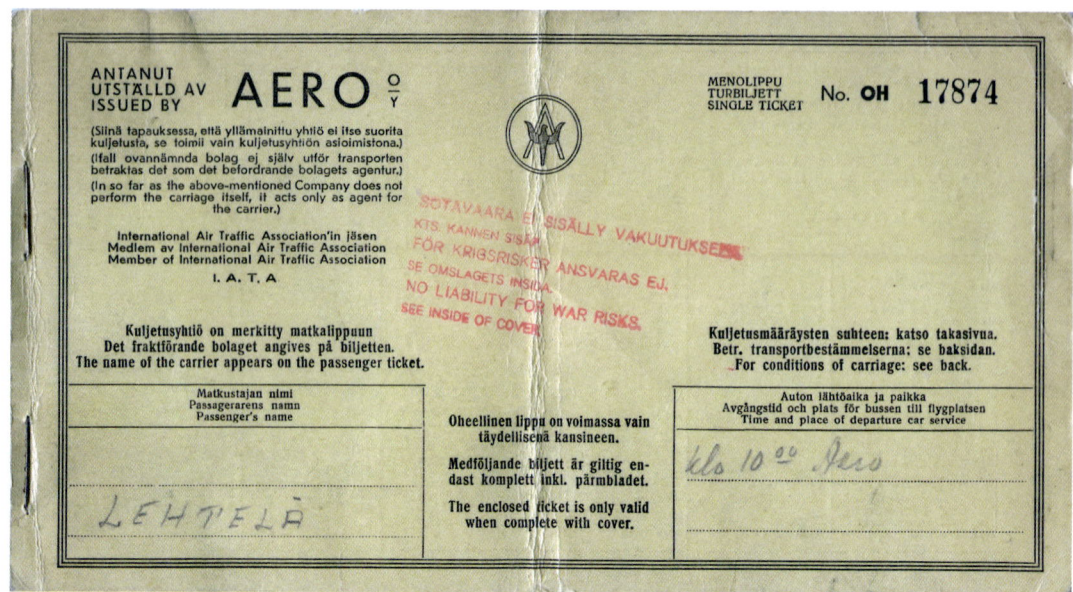

This Aero Oy ticket clearly states the airline is not responsible for war risks. (Finnish Aviation Museum)

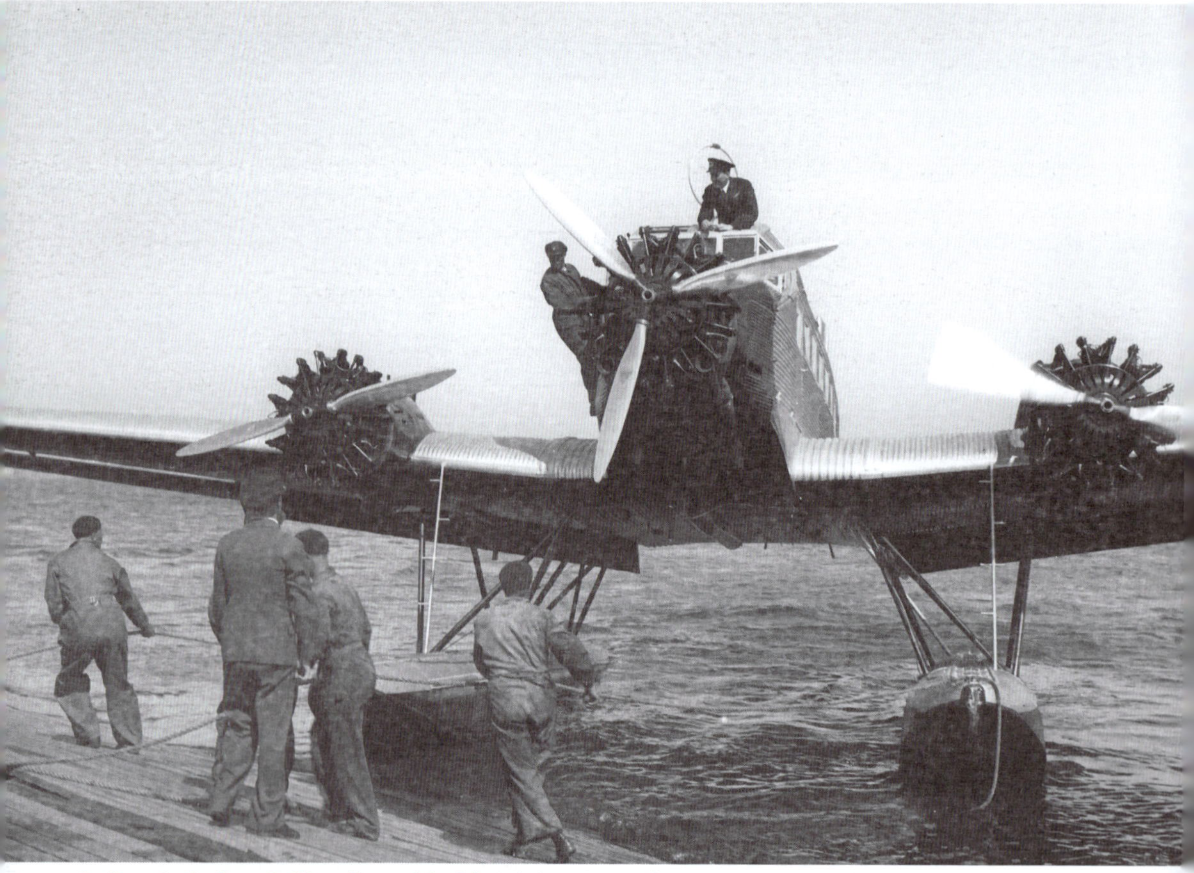

An Aero Oy Junkers Ju 52 on floats. (Finnish Aviation Museum)

Passengers on board an Aero Oy Ju 52. (Finnish Aviation Museum)

Right: A Ju 52 ready for departure. (Finnish Aviation Museum).

Below: For its domestic services, Aero Oy obtained some DH89 Dragon Rapides. (Finnish Aviation Museum, Eklöf Tor collection)

Above: The Dragon Rapide was the first non-German aircraft to enter the fleet of Aero Oy. (Finnish Aviation Museum, Eklöf Tor collection)

Left: A Dragon Rapide of Veljekset Karhumäki. (Finnish Aviation Museum)

Below: Two of the six Dragon Rapides in the Veljekset Karhumäki fleet. (Finnish Aviation Museum)

Chapter 2

Flying in Wartime

The war in Finland can, by no means, be compared to the war years in other European countries, as it had different origins. In 1809, the Russian Empire had taken Finland from Sweden during the Finnish War. Finland had entered into a personal union with the Russian Empire as a grand duchy with extensive autonomy. On 6 December 1917, during the Russian Civil War, the Finnish parliament declared independence from Russia, which was accepted by the Bolshevik regime of the Soviet Union. In January 1918, the Finnish parliament ordered General Carl Mannerheim to use local Finnish White Guards to disarm Finnish Red Guards and Russian troops in the country, leading to the Finnish Civil War. After peace negotiations, German troops intervened in Finland and occupied Helsinki. The Red faction was defeated, and survivors were subjected to a reign of terror. The Finnish government, led by Prime Minister Juho Kusti Paasikivi, pursued a pro-German policy and sought to annex Russian Karelia, which had a Finnish-speaking majority, although the area was never part of Finland. These events at the beginning of the 20th century resulted in new borders between Russia and Finland. The Finnish government abandoned its claims of Eastern Karelia, but some elements in Finland maintained the dream of a Greater Finland, which would include Karelia. Also, the proximity of the Finnish border to Leningrad (now St Petersburg) caused worry with the Soviet leadership. When Nazi Germany and the Soviet Union signed the Molotov–Ribbentrop Pact on 23 August 1939, a secret clause in the agreement marked Finland as part of the Soviet sphere of influence. On 12 October, negotiations between the Soviet Union and Finland started concerning parts of Finnish territory, but no agreement was reached. On 26 November, the Soviet Union accused the Finnish army of shelling the village of Mainila, but, in fact, the Soviets had shelled their own village to create an excuse to withdraw from their non-aggression pact with Finland. On 30 November, the Soviet Union attacked Finland. That day, Soviet aircraft bombed Helsinki. The final aim of the Soviet Union was to annex Finland.[1] As Helsinki was no longer safe, all flights to Stockholm were temporarily operated from Vaasa and Turku, while civil aviation was placed under military control. Almost half of the wartime passengers were children, evacuated to Sweden. Part of the civil aviation fleet was also requisitioned by the Finnish military. Of course, the planned Helsinki Olympics were cancelled, and Aero never took delivery of the Focke Wulf Condors it had ordered. On 13 March 1940, the Moscow Peace Treaty was signed after an ultimatum from the Soviet Union with a 48-hour time limit. When the Winter War was over, Finland was forced to cede land in its eastern Karelian sector to the Soviet Union. Aero Oy re-established air services and, from April 1940, resumed flights to Tallinn and Stockholm. On the domestic network, the airline started up the 'Lapland Express' to the northern city of Petsamo, in addition to more than a dozen other destinations.

The period of peace would not last very long, however. On 22 June 1941, Germany launched Operation *Barbarossa* and invaded the Soviet Union. A few days later, the Soviet Union launched an air raid against Finnish cities, after which Finland declared war and allowed German troops to begin offensive warfare against the Soviet Union, using Finnish territory. The resulting war was known as the Continuation War. Once again, civil aviation was put under military control and airlines operated their flights from the Pori airport, instead of Helsinki. Even after the United States and the Soviet Union became involved in hostilities with Germany, and in spite of fuel shortages, Aero Oy continued to operate services to Rovaniemi, Stockholm and even Berlin. During the war, and as Finland was a nominal German ally,

Aero Oy could obtain two Douglas DC-2 aircraft from Lufthansa. The aircraft had been seized previously from Czechoslovakia, when Germany had invaded that country two years earlier.

On 16 March 1944, US President Franklin D. Roosevelt called for Finland to disassociate itself from Nazi Germany. A few months later, the Red Army launched a major offensive against Finland. The offensive was fought to a standstill in the Battle of Tali–Ihantala, but the Finnish resources were exhausted. After the Soviet offensive, Finnish President Risto Ryti resigned from office. As no elections could be held, the parliament selected Marshal of Finland Carl Gustaf Emil Mannerheim (Finnish commander-in-chief) as president and charged him with negotiating peace. Soon, however, the Finnish front would become a sideshow for Moscow, as the Red Army was in a race to reach Berlin before the Western Allies. Most Soviet troops were transferred from the Finnish front. An armistice with the Soviet Union was signed on 19 September 1944. (The final peace treaty was only signed in Paris in 1947.)[2]

Once the armistice with the Soviet Union was signed, the Helsinki-Malmi airport was placed under Allied military control. Aero Oy, however, was allowed to resume operations to Turku, Mariehamn and Stockholm from Hyvinkää with its remaining fleet of five aircraft. Therefore, the airline had to operate its own bus service from downtown Helsinki to the airfield in Hyvinkää. A passenger terminal was built at Hyvinkää (which now is the residence of the Hyvinkää Aviation Club). The Allies banned all other commercial aviation from March until August of 1945. Gunnar Stänhle, the director of Aero Oy, was forced to resign by order of the Allied Control Commission, which cited his presumed sympathies for Nazi Germany during the war. For a short time, he was replaced by C. J. Ehrnrooth, who was soon replaced by Uolevi Raade. In the immediate months after the armistice, it was necessary to reorganise the airline in order to comply with Allied rules and regulations. A first board of directors was established in this period. In the period between 1945 and 1947, Aero Oy could only transport some 42,600 passengers.

It is clear that Aero Oy's business had suffered from the war like, of course, the entire Finnish economy. Finnish investment capital was scarce after the war, and Aero was forced to turn to the government to fund new equipment. In return for its financial backing, the Finnish government was allowed to acquire 70 per cent of the Aero shares. The remainder was held by banks, other companies and private citizens. Through the Finnish Ministry of Supply, Aero purchased several surplus American C-47s and asked Fokker in Holland to convert them to their civilian equivalent, the DC-3. The aircraft joined the fleet in May 1947 and received the new livery with the Finnish Air Lines title. For the first time, Aero Oy also introduced flight attendants on its flights. By 1949, the airline had retired all its DC-2s, Junkers and Dragon Rapide aircraft to replace them with more modern equipment. By that time, international services could be resumed. On 3 November 1947, Aero Oy resumed scheduled flights to Stockholm, followed by Copenhagen in March 1948. In July 1948, Amsterdam was added to the route map. The Amsterdam route was dubbed the 'Tulip Line' and was operated twice weekly from Helsinki with stops in Norrköping and Copenhagen. A return ticket cost 587 guilders, and 870 passengers flew on the route during that first half year. From April 1955, Amsterdam became an important stop on the routes to Paris and London.

The Helsinki Olympic Games were rescheduled for 1952. In preparation, Aero Oy reconfigured its fleet and redesigned the new Helsinki Airport near Seutula. When, in 1952, the airline had transported more than 100,000 passengers, the need for larger and more modern aircraft became clear. It was decided to obtain the Convair 340, which had room for 44 passengers and offered better comfort thanks to the pressurised cabin. The even more advanced Convair 440 Metropolitan was also added to the fleet. In 1953, the company introduced the Finnair brand in its advertising materials and on its aircraft, but the company's official name did not change.

Above: During World War Two, Aero Oy obtained two Douglas DC-2 aircraft from Germany. The Aero Oy logo was replaced by the Finnish Air Lines title. (Finnish Aviation Museum/Paldan)

Right: After the war, Aero Oy obtained several Douglas DC-3 aircraft. The Aero Oy logo was still used on the tail, but 'Finnish Air Lines' was marked on the fuselage. (Helsinki City Museum)

Below: Aero Oy staff and passengers in front of a DC-3. (Finnair)

Above: **An Aero Oy DC-3. For marketing purposes, the name 'Finnish Air Lines' was replaced by the 'Finnair' title, but officially the company kept its old name. (Finnish Aviation Museum)**

Left: **A Convair 340 seen at Heathrow Airport. The introduction of the type made the introduction of international flights possible. (Finnair)**

Below: **The inaugural flight to London took place with a Convair. (Finnair)**

Above: A Convair 340 seen at Oulu airport. (Saarinen National Board of Antiquities)

Right: Cabin crews were introduced in the early 1950s when Convairs entered the fleet. (Finnish Aviation Museum)

Below: This old postcard, issued by the airline, shows its Convair 440 Metropolitan. (Finnair)

Chapter 3
The Jet Age

Just like Aero Oy, Karhumäki Airways (Kar Air) suffered during the war years. In June 1951, scheduled services were resumed with a fleet of four Douglas DC-3s and two Convair CV-440s. In the beginning, only domestic flights were operated to Jyväskylä, Vaasa and Sundsvall. The first international flight – to Stockholm – took place in the last months of 1951. However, because of its limited fleet Karhumäki Airways was, at that stage, not a real competitor for Aero Oy.

Aero Oy used the same type of aircraft as its competitor but was faster in expanding its network. When three CV-340s arrived in Finland (later followed by the larger 440s), the airline started up services to Stockholm, Copenhagen and Amsterdam. In 1953, the Convairs started flying a Helsinki–Copenhagen–Düsseldorf route. After opening up routes to Paris (in 1953) and London (in 1954), Aero Oy became the first Western airline since the end of the war to start flying to Moscow. The number of domestic destinations increased and, by 1957, Aero Oy's domestic network was among the densest in Europe. This network was mainly serviced by DC-3s, but, by March 1955, the passenger volume had grown to such an extent that all the Convairs were pressed into temporary service. Expansion was so rapid that the airline decided to set up a committee to select a successor to the CV-340s and CV-440s. This committee recommended the French Sud Aviation SE-210 Caravelle passenger jet. This was the first commercial jet aircraft to be designed for short- and medium-haul flights. In January 1958, the airline ordered three aircraft for delivery in spring 1960. Compared to Aero Oy's earlier aircraft, the Caravelle was completely different. The two Rolls-Royce Avon jet engines delivered a cruising speed of 800km/h, yet the cabin noise level was remarkably low. Aero Oy's Caravelles were delivered with 16 first class seats and 57 economy class seats. Aero Oy became the first airline in the world to operate a passenger jet with a flight crew of two instead of the normal three. The first Caravelle arrived on 21 February 1960. On 1 April, the aircraft went into service on the Helsinki–Copenhagen–Cologne–Frankfurt–Helsinki–Stockholm route. Later, jet services followed to Hamburg, Amsterdam, London, Paris, Zürich and Malmö. In February 1962, Aero Oy received its fourth Caravelle, but this time, it was the heavier Caravelle II, equipped with more powerful engines. (Later, the first three Caravelles in the fleet would be converted to this improved Caravelle version.)

It was Aero Oy's intention to also operate the Caravelles on winter charter flights to Majorca, the Canary Islands and Rimini, as the arrival of the new jets had increased the airline's capacity. At that time, however, the IATA regulations prevented Aero from directly operating charter flights. Therefore, Aero Oy created a subsidiary, Polar Air, to handle this business. Apart from a managing director and a sales representative, the company had no organisation of its own and all flights were handled by Aero Oy. At the same time, the international network was further expanded to include Leningrad, Athens, Dubrovnik and Brussels. Considering the rapid expansion, Aero Oy decided to open the Finnair Aviation College to train pilots who could be recruited out of the Finnish Air Force. The college opened its doors on 1 January 1964.

While Aero Oy was expanding its operations, Karhumäki Airways was reorganised as Kar-Air Oy and obtained a single Douglas DC-6 with which charter flights to Southern Europe were started. However, when two Kar-Air Metropolitans were damaged in hard landings and had to be taken out of service for a while, the airline experienced severe financial difficulties. Aero Oy came to the rescue and obtained a 27 per cent stake in Kar-Air. Polar Air's Caravelle charter flights to Southern Europe were transferred to Kar-Air, but the 'Polar Air' brand remained in use on later charter flights to Israel. This way, Finnair – via Polar Air and Kar-Air – moved European charter flight traffic into the jet age, as the company was one of the first to use jet aircraft for European charters.

The purchase of the Caravelles proved to be a magic moment in the history of Aero Oy. Between 1964 and 1967, the airline took delivery of eight Super Caravelles and, by 1967, jets were flying 95 per cent of the company's scheduled traffic. On 15 December 1961, a Caravelle had been operated for the first time on a domestic route, linking Helsinki with Oulu. The aircraft were also leased to other airlines, and in the summer of 1962, Finnair operated the type on the Frankfurt–Paris route on behalf of Lufthansa.

The 1960s and the introduction of jet equipment marked a period of major change for the airline. In the autumn of 1966, the government began the construction of a new terminal building for Helsinki Airport, which was completed in the spring of 1969. Then, at the beginning of 1968, Aero Oy launched a new company logo and officially changed its name to Finnair Oy. That year, for the first time, the airline carried more than one million passengers. Finnair also laid plans to expand into the hotel and travel agency business, as part of an effort to achieve greater control over all aspects of the tourism industry.[1]

On 1 January 1966, Aero Oy had opened an office in New York. In order to start up transatlantic services, the airline placed orders for two Douglas DC-8-62CF aircraft, designed for exceptionally long-range flights. The first of these aircraft arrived in Helsinki on 8 February 1969 and was used for a short while on international charter routes. Finnair DC-8 flights from Helsinki via Copenhagen and Amsterdam to New York began on 15 May 1969. Though the stops were not required, as the Dash 62 variant of the DC-8 was capable of flying from Europe to the US with fuel to spare, the additional stops helped the airline to earn some extra revenue on the route by transporting freight.[2] The new ability to connect Helsinki and New York created an opportunity for Finnair to be the airborne ambassador of Finnish culture to the US via its onboard service. To this effect, trained flight attendants, called 'Finn Hostesses', wearing designer uniforms served first-class passengers champagne and caviar in specially designed glasses and flatware, some of which is still featured today in Finnair's business class. Two years later, continuing its association with Douglas, Finnair added the smaller DC-9 aircraft to its fleet and opened new routes to Lisbon and East Berlin. In the meantime, Finnair had introduced non-smoking cabins on the London route. In March 1972, such sections would become standard practice on all Finnair flights.

Just Like Aero Oy, its competitor Kar-Air was using DC-3 aircraft on mainly domestic routes. (Helsinki City Museum)

Above: A Kar-Air DC-3 at the Helsinki Airport in 1950. (Arvo Kajantie/Wikimedia Commons Licence)

Left: Kar-Air also used the Convair 440, just like Aero Oy. (Helsinki City Museum)

Below: A Kar-Air Convair Metropolitan at Helsinki Airport. (Helsinki City Museum)

A Kar-Air Convair Metropolitan is being prepared for a next flight. (Finnish Aviation Museum)

Finnair entered the jet-age with Caravelles and Super Caravelles. (Clipperarctic/Wikimedia Commons Licence)

Passengers leaving a Finnair Super Caravelle. (Helsinki City Museum)

Left: A Finnair Super Caravelle at Helsinki Airport. (Helsinki City Museum)

Below: Finnair operated its transatlantic routes with DC-8 aircraft, often via Amsterdam or Brussels. (Jozef Mols collection)

A Finnair DC-8 ready for departure. (Finnair)

Right: This old Finnair photo shows the DC-8 when it was introduced on transatlantic routes. (Finnair)

Below: This DC-8 arrives at Helsinki airport. (Dean Faulkner/Wikimedia Commons Licence)

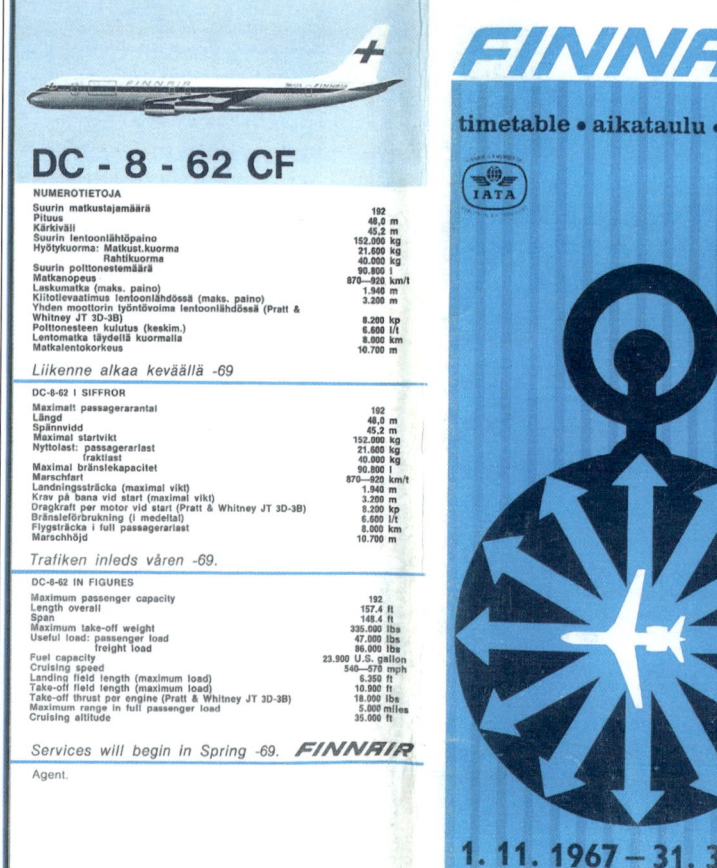

FINNAIR

timetable • aikataulu • tidtabell

DC - 8 - 62 CF

NUMEROTIETOJA

Suurin matkustajamäärä	192
Pituus	48,0 m
Kärkiväli	45,2 m
Suurin lentoonlähtöpaino	152.000 kg
Hyötykuorma: Matkust.kuorma	21.600 kg
Rahtikuorma	40.000 kg
Suurin polttonestemäärä	90.800 l
Matkanopeus	870—920 km/t
Laskumatka (maks. paino)	1.940 m
Kiitotievaatimus lentoonlähdössä (maks. paino)	3.200 m
Yhden moottorin työntövoima lentoonlähdössä (Pratt & Whitney JT 3D-3B)	8.200 kp
Polttonesteen kulutus (keskim.)	6.600 l/t
Lentomatka täydellä kuormalla	8.000 km
Matkalentokorkeus	10.700 m

Liikenne alkaa keväällä -69

DC-8-62 I SIFFROR

Maximalt passagerarantal	192
Längd	48,0 m
Spännvidd	45,2 m
Maximal startvikt	152.000 kg
Nyttolast: passagerarlast	21.600 kg
fraktlast	40.000 kg
Maximal bränslekapacitet	90.800 l
Marschfart	870—920 km/t
Landningssträcka (maximal vikt)	1.940 m
Krav på bana vid start (maximal vikt)	3.200 m
Dragkraft per motor vid start (Pratt & Whitney JT 3D-3B)	8.200 kp
Bränsleförbrukning (i medeltal)	6.600 l/t
Flygsträcka i full passagerarlast	8.000 km
Marschhöjd	10.700 m

Trafiken inleds våren -69.

DC-8-62 IN FIGURES

Maximum passenger capacity	192
Length overall	157.4 ft
Span	148.4 ft
Maximum take-off weight	335.000 lbs
Useful load: passenger load	47.000 lbs
freight load	86.000 lbs
Fuel capacity	23.900 U.S. gallon
Cruising speed	540—570 mph
Landing field length (maximum load)	6.350 ft
Take-off field length (maximum load)	10.900 ft
Take-off thrust per engine (Pratt & Whitney JT 3D-3B)	18.000 lbs
Maximum range in full passenger load	5.000 miles
Cruising altitude	35.000 ft

Services will begin in Spring -69. **FINNAIR**

Agent.

IATA

1. 11. 1967 – 31. 3. 1968

Above: **Inaugural flight to New York by a DC-8. (Finnair)**

Left: **This Finnair timetable from 1967 shows the technical details of the new DC-8. (Alan Bushell collection)**

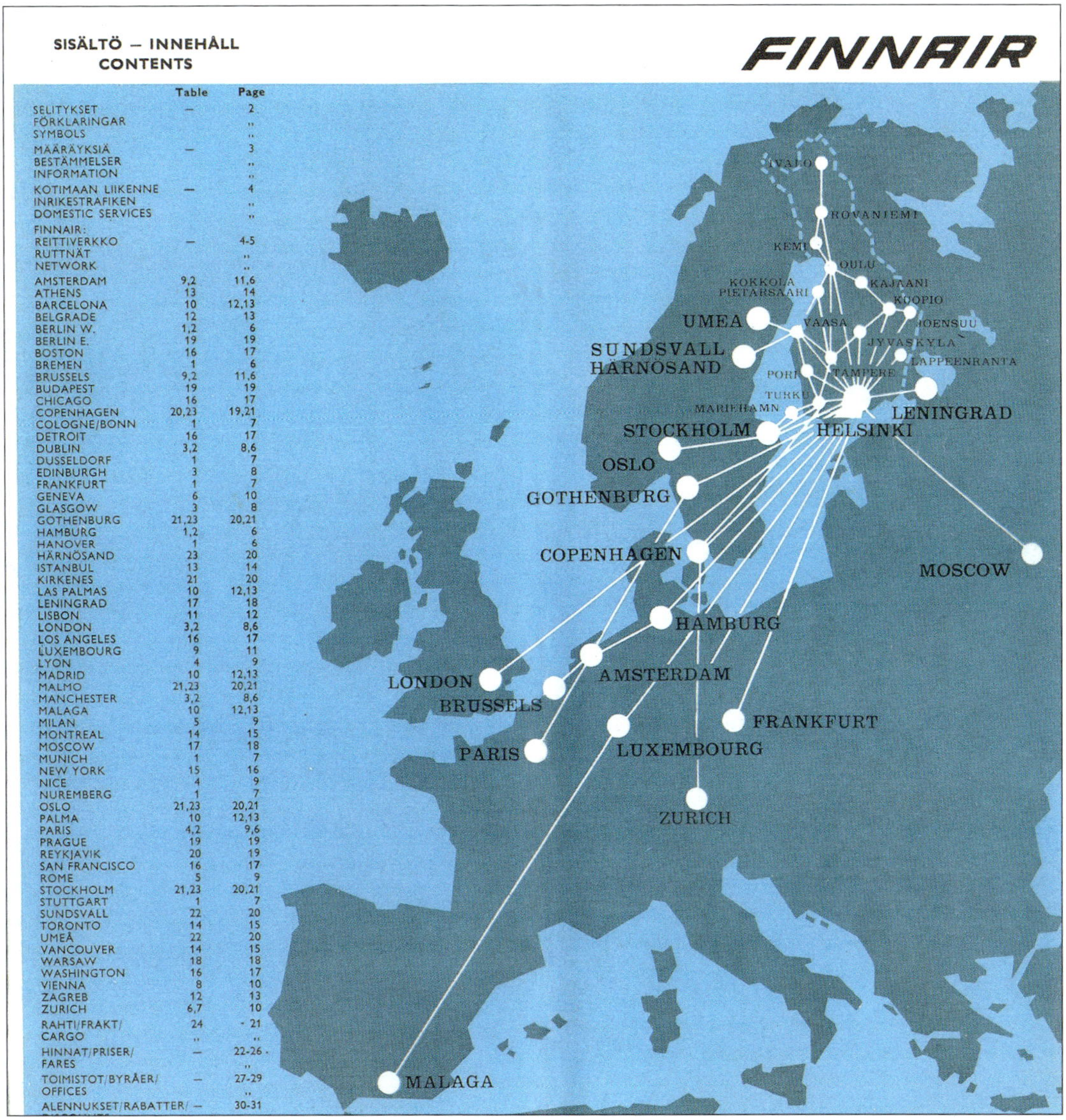

SISÄLTÖ – INNEHÅLL
CONTENTS

FINNAIR

	Table	Page
SELITYKSET	—	2
FÖRKLARINGAR		,,
SYMBOLS		,,
MÄÄRÄYKSIÄ	—	3
BESTÄMMELSER		,,
INFORMATION		,,
KOTIMAAN LIIKENNE	—	4
INRIKESTRAFIKEN		,,
DOMESTIC SERVICES		,,
FINNAIR:		
REITTIVERKKO	—	4-5
RUTTNÄT		,,
NETWORK		,,
AMSTERDAM	9,2	11,6
ATHENS	13	14
BARCELONA	10	12,13
BELGRADE	12	13
BERLIN W.	1,2	6
BERLIN E.	19	19
BOSTON	16	17
BREMEN	1	6
BRUSSELS	9,2	11,6
BUDAPEST	19	19
CHICAGO	16	17
COPENHAGEN	20,23	19,21
COLOGNE/BONN	1	7
DETROIT	16	17
DUBLIN	3,2	8,6
DUSSELDORF	1	7
EDINBURGH	3	8
FRANKFURT	1	7
GENEVA	6	10
GLASGOW	3	8
GOTHENBURG	21,23	20,21
HAMBURG	1,2	6
HANOVER	1	6
HÄRNÖSAND	23	20
ISTANBUL	13	14
KIRKENES	21	20
LAS PALMAS	10	12,13
LENINGRAD	17	18
LISBON	11	12
LONDON	3,2	8,6
LOS ANGELES	16	17
LUXEMBOURG	9	11
LYON	4	9
MADRID	10	12,13
MALMO	21,23	20,21
MANCHESTER	3,2	8,6
MALAGA	10	12,13
MILAN	5	9
MONTREAL	14	15
MOSCOW	17	18
MUNICH	1	7
NEW YORK	15	16
NICE	4	9
NUREMBERG	1	7
OSLO	21,23	20,21
PALMA	10	12,13
PARIS	4,2	9,6
PRAGUE	19	19
REYKJAVIK	20	19
SAN FRANCISCO	16	17
ROME	5	9
STOCKHOLM	21,23	20,21
STUTTGART	1	7
SUNDSVALL	22	20
TORONTO	14	15
UMEÅ	22	20
VANCOUVER	14	15
WARSAW	18	18
WASHINGTON	16	17
VIENNA	8	10
ZAGREB	12	13
ZURICH	6,7	10
RAHTI/FRAKT/	24	- 21
CARGO	,,	,,
HINNAT/PRISER/	—	22-26
FARES		,,
TOIMISTOT/BYRÅER/	—	27-29
OFFICES		,,
ALENNUKSET/RABATTER/	—	30-31

IVALO
ROVANIEMI
KEMI
OULU
KOKKOLA
PIETARSAARI
KAJAANI
KUOPIO
UMEA
VAASA
JOENSUU
SUNDSVALL
HÄRNÖSAND
JYVÄSKYLÄ
LAPPEENRANTA
PORI
TAMPERE
TURKU
MARIEHAMN
LENINGRAD
STOCKHOLM
HELSINKI
OSLO
GOTHENBURG
COPENHAGEN
MOSCOW
HAMBURG
AMSTERDAM
LONDON
BRUSSELS
FRANKFURT
PARIS
LUXEMBOURG
ZURICH
MALAGA

Above: The 1967 timetable also shows the route-network. (Alan Bushell collection)

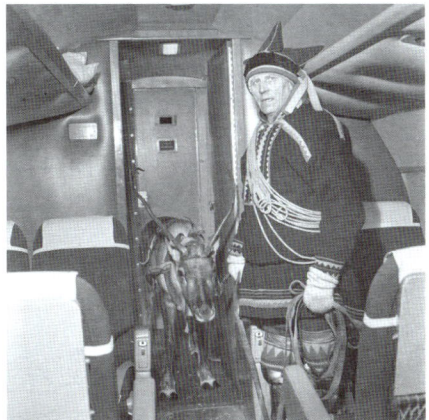

Right: Starting in 1962, Finnair also started to promote tourism to the northern regions of the country. (National Board of Antiquities)

Left: With this photo, Finnair made publicity for its flights to Finnish Lapland. (National Board of Antiquities)

Below: While trying to get better control over the Finnish tourism sector, Finnair also promoted its own tours and flights to Lapland. (National Board of Antiquities)

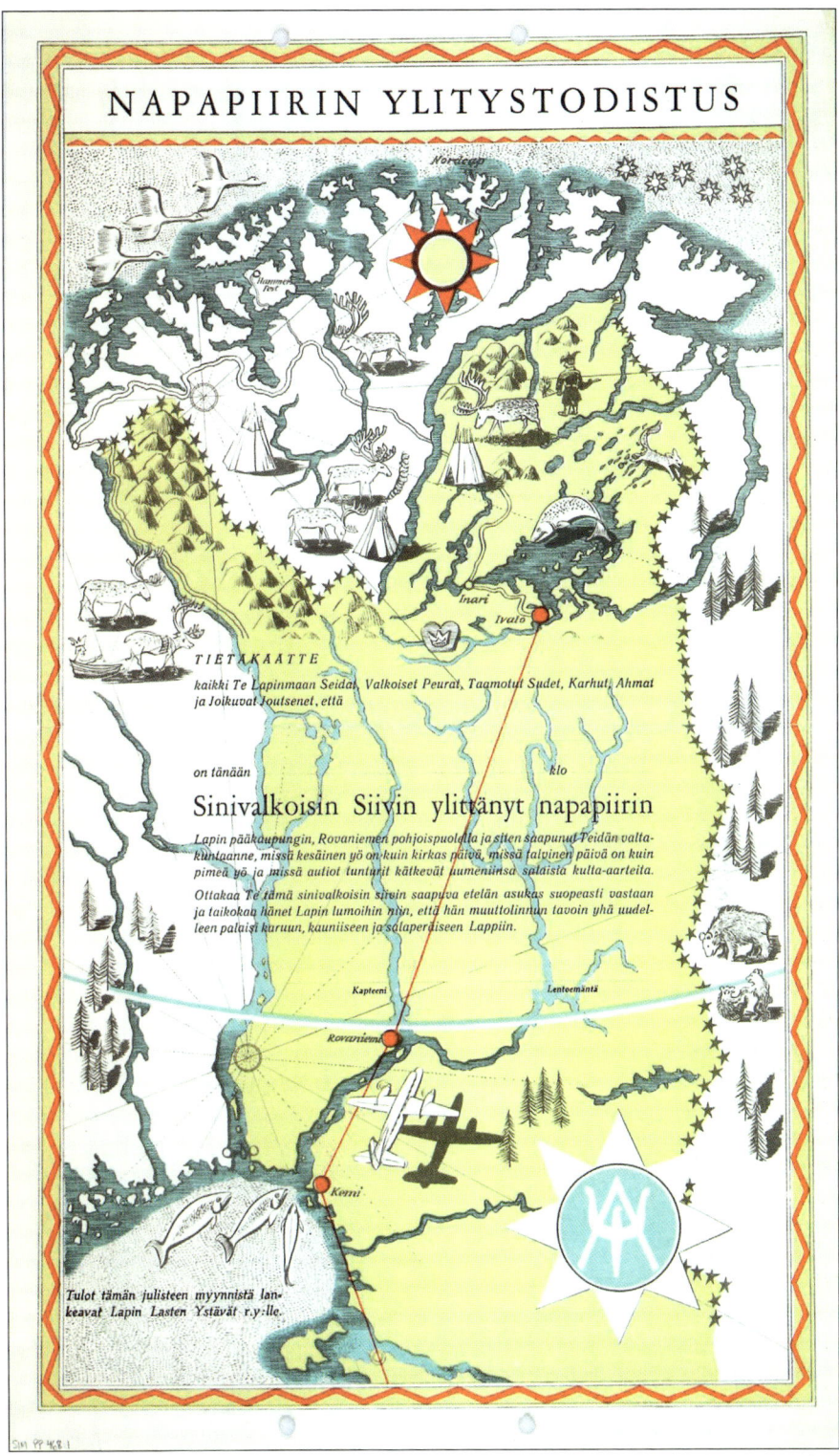

Passengers crossing the Polar Circle received this certificate. (National Board of Antiquities)

Chapter 4

Intercontinental Operations

The first DC-9-10 arrived in January 1971 and would serve until September 1983. The same year, two more aircraft of the same type would follow. Later on, between 1972 and 1983, another six of these aircraft joined the fleet. When the domestic market reacted favourably to the introduction of these jets, Finnair Oy decided to obtain larger versions of the same basic model. Several DC-9-40s arrived in Finland between 1981 and 1983, followed by DC-9-50s between 1976 and 2003. In total, Finnair would use 27 aircraft of the DC-9 family. The larger models would become the backbone of the airline's European operations but would, in time, also replace the smaller DC-9-10s on Scandinavian routes.

When Finnair had to abandon the Convair 440 Metropolitan by the end of the 1970s, as by then it was considered obsolete, it was decided the airliner needed propeller aircraft, smaller than the DC-9, for its short-haul routes.[1] At the same time, the Finnish Air Force was looking for a replacement for its fleet of DC-3s. The military considered several aircraft, including the Antonov An-32, Fokker F27, CASA C-212 and de Havilland Canada DHC-7. In the end, the Air Force decided to lease two Fokker F27s. In 1980, Finnair also obtained its first F27-200 Friendship in Iceland. The aircraft served domestic routes until its retirement in 1988, when it was replaced by ATR 42-200s. The same year, a second F27 (also obtained in Iceland) joined the fleet, followed by a third one that remained in the fleet until 1988.

Of course, Finnair was also considering expanding its intercontinental network. Therefore, the airline ordered two wide-bodied McDonnell Douglas DC-10-30s. The first of these aircraft arrived in Finland on 4 February 1975 and made its first commercial flight ten days later on the route from Helsinki to Las Palmas. On 27 March 1975, the aircraft started transatlantic flights. In November 1976, flights to Bangkok began, and they were continued until the winter season of 1982. They were followed by numerous routes to the Middle East. In 1977, Finnair also started offering pilgrim flights to Mecca. That same year, Montreal was added to the transatlantic route network.

In the meantime, Finnair had increased its participation in Kar-Air to a majority holding of 50 per cent and asked the carrier to cease domestic flights. Instead, the airline was ordered to concentrate on charter flights, mainly to the Mediterranean holiday resorts. For that purpose, Finnair had bought Douglas DC-6 aircraft to be operated by Kar-Air. The DC-6 remained the backbone of the Kar-Air passenger fleet until 1975, when the jet age was joined with the introduction of the 189-seat DC-8. One DC-6 was reconfigured with a swing tail unit for cargo transport and would stay with the airline until 1980. It mainly operated freight flights for Finnair to the UK and other European destinations. Over the following years, Kar-Air (now rebranded as Karair) had to reduce its fleet because charter contracts with Finnair were terminated.

Also on the domestic market, Finnair created Finnaviation in 1979. It was formed from the reorganisation of Wihuri Oy Finnwings (which had started services in 1950 as Lentohuolto Oy) and its merging with Nordair Oy. Finnair had a dominant 60 per cent stake in the new carrier. Scheduled services began in October 1979. Karair provided two Embraer EMB-110s to the new company. Finnaviation was to provide feeder services for Finnair and take over domestic routes that were no longer profitable for Finnair. Besides this, Finnaviation also operated ambulance, charter and mail flights. By the summer of 1980, when Finnair had increased its participation to 70 per cent, Finnaviation's network included seven airports in Finland and three in Sweden. In 1986, the airline took delivery of Saab 340 regional airliners in combi-version, which replaced the EMB-110s. During the day, the aircraft were operated on passenger flights, while at night, they were used as freighter for Finland Post.

Notwithstanding the activities on the domestic and regional market, Finnair had also been expanding its long-haul network. In 1981, the airline had opened routes to Seattle and Los Angeles. It also became the first operator to fly non-stop from Western Europe to Japan, operating the Helsinki–Tokyo routes with a modified DC-10-30ER. Until then, flights had to be routed via Moscow or Anchorage due to Soviet airspace restrictions, but Finnair circumvented these by flying directly north from Helsinki over the North Pole and back south through the Bering Strait, avoiding Soviet airspace. The decision to use this route was taken under pressure from Japan Airlines and the Japanese authorities, although Finnair got authorisations from the Soviet Union to use a route via Moscow. It would soon become clear that the transpolar route was shorter and, therefore, more comfortable for the passengers. As a result, the new route would become one of Finnair's many advertorial topics. In June 1985, a second weekly flight on the route was introduced. The DC-10-30ER, fitted with larger fuel tanks, flew the transpolar route in 13 hours. The routes with a stopover in Moscow, flown by Aeroflot, SAS and British Airways took the same amount of time, but most other carriers operated the route via Anchorage, which took up to 16 hours. For a while, Finnair could enjoy this competitive advantage until, in 1986, Soviet regulators cleared the way for Air France and Japan Airlines to fly nonstop Paris–Tokyo services over Soviet airspace. This way, Finnair lost its advantage that year.

In April 1983, Finnair put the DC-9 Super 82 in service on its European trunk routes where they replaced the older DC-9-51. Also in 1983, the last Super Caravelle left the airline fleet, having served for nearly 23 years. The first two McDonnell Douglas MD-83 aircraft ordered by Finnair – the first European airline to do so – arrived in Finland on 27 June 1985. The aircraft were used on the longest European and domestic scheduled flights. The same year, Finnair signed a contract with the French-Italian ATR group for the purchase of five ATR 42 turboprop aircraft, intended for the short domestic routes. In order to further expand its activities in the travel market, Finnair decided to set up a new independent profit centre ATRAIMEN (Automatic Travel Information), which offered a range of travel services and products, such as hotel and travel agency services and reservation systems 'at the touch of the button'.[2]

Besides its advantages on the Polar route, Finnair also benefited greatly from the unusual relationship between Finland and the Soviet Union. Indeed, both countries shared many parallel interests. Finnair was offered greater access to Eastern Bloc cities and airspace than many other Western airline companies, and it succeeded in using this as a corporate asset. One result of this relationship was a growth in air freight, which compelled the airline to invest heavily in a new air cargo facility at Helsinki-Vantaa Airport in 1986. Other investments included the set-up of a training school for commercial pilots in Pori. In 1986, the school obtained a DC-10 flight deck simulator to enhance crew training. The acquisition, amounting to millions of Finnish marks (FIM), had become necessary as a result of the company's expanded DC-10 fleet and its growing number of long-distance routes. An MD-80 simulator was later added to the equipment of the school. In 1987, Finnair received the first of its eight MD-87 aircraft for use on mainly European scheduled routes. The last aircraft of this type would arrive in April 1991. Finnair's first Airbus A300B4-203 had already arrived in Helsinki in 1986. Five days after its arrival, the wide-bodied aircraft flew in Karair's colours to Lanzarote in the Canary Islands. A second aircraft of the same type arrived in March 1987 and was used by Finnair on scheduled flights to two new European destinations: Münich and Geneva.

Not all of Finnair's activities were successful, however. Finnair flights to Cairo (introduced on 3 November 1979) and Baghdad (introduced on 3 April 1980) had to be suspended because of the outbreak of the Iran-Iraq War. The Helsinki–Luxemburg–Malaga route also came under pressure. Finnair had introduced this route with a stop in Luxemburg, as this small country was becoming an important centre for 'low-cost airlines' like Loftleidir and Air Bahama. It was Finnair's intention to offer lower fares on the Luxemburg–Malaga sector, but the Spanish authorities withdrew the right to operate between Luxemburg and Malaga to avoid it competing with Spanish airlines, which compelled the company to discontinue the route. Flights to Amman in Jordan (introduced in April 1982) were also discontinued as unprofitable in January 1983. Successes in Eastern Europe came under pressure as well. Political changes in the Soviet Union after 1986 opened up Eastern European destinations to more Western airlines and shifted Soviet business alliances to Germany, where greater investment capital was available. Nevertheless, Finnair managed to retain its position as the gateway airport to the Soviet Union and the Baltic states. This position was strengthened later in 1989, after Finnair backed the opening of the Strand Intercontinental in Helsinki and the Savoy Hotel in Moscow. In addition, Finnair had to face high-cost structures, which led the company to undertake a series of cost-cutting moves and reduce the number of employees by 10 per cent beginning in 1990.

In 1988, Finnair launched its Helsinki–Beijing route, becoming the first Western European carrier to fly non-stop to China. Earlier, in December 1985, Finnair had already opened a new route from Helsinki to Singapore via Bangkok. The start of these services to Southeast Asia had become necessary, particularly because of the strongly growing trade links between Finland and the region. On the outbound flight, first and business class passengers were given a summary of the financial and business news in the press of the region. Similarly, on the return flight back to Europe, passengers received a summary of news from Finland and the rest of Europe. To further enhance its service level, Finnair announced it would be the first airline in the world to acquire satellite telephones for its DC-10 aircraft, enabling passengers to call from the aircraft via satellite to anywhere in the world.[3] When, in 1989, Finnair decided to list its shares on the Helsinki Stock Exchange, the airline was transporting an average of five million passengers per year.

For its subsidiary Kar-Air, Finnair obtained Douglas DC-6 aircraft, which were used for charter flights. (Finnish Aviation Museum)

Above: A Kar-Air DC-6, which was leased from Finnair. (Hielm Borje – Finnish Aviation Museum)

Right: One of Kar-Air's DC-6B aircraft was converted into a swing-tail model and was used by Finnair for cargo flights. (Finnish Aviation Museum)

Below: Karair's DC-6B aircraft were replaced by DC-8 equipment. (Rod Hodgkins/Wikimedia Commons Licence)

Above: The Douglas DC-9-10 was introduced on domestic routes. (Jozef Mols)

Left: Once the DC-9-10 had been accepted by the public, the DC-9-40 was introduced. (Rod Hodgkins/Wikimedia Commons Licence)

Below: The DC-9-50 was also used by Finnair on European routes. (Raymond Zammit)

Above left: The Douglas DC-10 made it possible to launch routes to the Far East. (Helsinki City Museum)

Above right: The DC-10 was also used on transatlantic routes. (Helsinki City Museum)

Thanks to its large cargo holds, the DC-10 was very useful for Finnair's cargo division. (Helsinki City Museum)

Above: A DC-10-30 ready to leave Helsinki. (Clipperarctic/ Wikimedia Commons Licence)

Left: The Fokker F27 was selected to fly on Finnair's lighter domestic routes. (Jozef Mols collection)

Below: A Finnair Fokker F27 at Malmi Airport. (G B_NZ/ Wikimedia Commons Licence)

Above: Finnair's subsidiary Finnaviation used a fleet of Saab 340 aircraft on mainly domestic flights. (Jozef Mols)

Right: A Finnair DC-9 Super 82 (MD-82) in flight. (Finnair)

Below: An MD-82 waiting for its passengers to board. (Jozef Mols)

Above: An MD-83 at Zürich Airport. (Jozef Mols collection)

Left: A Finnair MD-82 in flight. (Jozef Mols collection)

A Finnair MD-83 at Frankfurt Airport. (Jozef Mols collection)

The MD-87 also entered the Finnair fleet. (Aero Icarus/Wikimedia Commons Licence)

Finnair obtained two Airbus A-300 aircraft. (Finnish Aviation Museum)

Above left: Finnair's A-300s were leased to Karair. (Jozef Mols collection)

Above right: Finnair ordered five ATR 42 aircraft in 1985, the first of which arrived in 1988. (Pertti Sipila/ Wikimedia Commons Licence)

Chapter 5

The Official Airline of Santa Claus

T he first McDonnell Douglas MD-11 joined the fleet in December 1990, three years after being ordered by Finnair as a launch customer. The first flight with the new type went from Helsinki to Tenerife in the Canary Islands on 20 December 1990. One of the MD-11s was recruited for a very special mission, and it was painted with the special 'Official Airline of Santa Claus' scheme. Actually, Finnair had already used this logo much earlier. In 1984, Finnair flew in the livery of Santa Claus, and the company would become 'The Official Carrier of Santa Claus' four years later. According to Finnair, the heart of its relationship with Santa is the carrier's collaboration with the Santa Claus Foundation. This charity donates an annual present 'to the children of the world' together with the partners of Santa Claus and has an overall aim of improving the wellbeing of children all over the world. On the one hand, this means flying Santa on a goodwill tour of Europe and Asia with a major focus on China and Japan to visit preschools, kindergartens and hospitals to spread Christmas cheer. Of course, on the other hand, it is a great way of promoting tourism to the northern part of Finland and to bring visitors to the Santa Claus Village, which is located about 5 miles northeast of Rovaniemi and about 1.2 miles from the Rovaniemi Airport. In 1985, Rovaniemi was declared as an official hometown of Santa Claus. Rovaniemi had almost been completely destroyed in World War Two. In 1950, Eleanor Roosevelt, the widow of former US President Franklin D. Roosevelt, came to visit Rovaniemi to witness the rebuilding process. As she wanted to visit the Arctic Circle, Rovaniemi officials rushed to build a cabin near the city. The cabin marked the birth of Santa Claus Village and still stands today. Of course, the amusement park also attracts tourists wishing to see the Northern Lights, also known as Aurora Borealis, or to experience other Arctic adventures.

In 1986, two Airbus A300 wide-body aircraft had joined the Karair fleet, which were leased from Finnair and deployed on holiday charter flights. Finnair's plans with Karair changed, however, from 1989, when the first of six ATR 72 short-haul turboprop aircraft was added to the fleet, and the Airbus aircraft in turn left the fleet. From then, scheduled domestic passenger flights were operated on behalf of Finnair. In 1990, Finnair acquired further shares of Karair to hold a total of 90 per cent of the Karair stake, which was further increased to 97.6 per cent in 1993. This period was characterised by financial problems caused by the recession of the early 1990s, which led to Finnair announcing a full take-over of Karair in December 1995. Subsequently, the Karair fleet and the airline's operations were merged into Finnair, a move which was completed in September 1996. (However, in 2002, a court ruled the take-over was illegal, and Finnair was forced to salvage the remaining Karair stocks.)[1]

In the early 1990s, as a result of the recession during this period, Finnair teamed up with Scandinavian Airlines System (SAS), Austrian Airlines and Swissair in an attempt to establish the European Quality Alliance (EQA). In addition to codesharing and joint marketing, the alliance was largely based around technical issues and the members wanted to use the EQA brand as a 'seal of quality'. Additionally, it was the intention to pool financial resources for future aircraft purchases.

The project stagnated, however, mainly because Finnair felt that SAS's goal was to use Finnair as a feeder airline to SAS's hub at Copenhagen Airport.[2]

During the economic recession, Finnair accumulated losses of FIM 576m (£81.8m) between 1991 and 1993. Therefore, the airline had to launch some cost-cutting measures in 1991. It pulled back flights from the Mediterranean in response to the Persian Gulf crisis, but increased its number of flights to Portugal, which had become more popular as a tourist destination. The onset of the glasnost not only opened up new routes to Russia, but also allowed more direct flights to the Far East. Still, the company continued to reduce its work force as a means of remaining profitable.[3]

Another part of the company's strategy to remain profitable was to reduce the number of aircraft types it operated. Finnair began replacing its DC-9s with used MD-80 aircraft. A stock offering in January 1995 helped fund the purchases. This offering received much attention from European investment institutions and raised foreign ownership of Finnair from 5 to 16 per cent. In 1997, however, the airline's board voted to replace the MD-80s on its European routes with Airbus aircraft, an order to be worth FIM 2 billion (£284m). Finnair still operated a dozen DC-9s, and, in June 1998, announced it was retrofitting them with newly available hush kits to help reduce the disturbing noise close to airports. At the same time, the airline also decided to lease some Boeing 757s. In order to expand its cargo business, which accounted for about 13 per cent of the company's total turnover, the airline completed expansion work on its cargo terminal at the end of 1997.

In the meantime, Finnair had installed a second hub in Stockholm, which was also home to SAS's headquarters. Finnair fed the hub via codeshare agreements with other Scandinavian carriers and declared itself Stockholm's official airline.[4] Together with Maersk Air, Finnair competed on one of SAS's most lucrative routes between Copenhagen and Stockholm. This only happened after SAS began flying from Frankfurt into Maersk's home base in Billund (Denmark).

Slowly, competitors were taking away from Finnair's domestic market share. In 1993, Juhani Pakari and his father started Finncomm Airlines as an air taxi business, flying light aircraft to remote airstrips that were not served by other airlines. Seeking to acquire an Air Operator's Certificate (AOC), necessary to start up scheduled flights, Fincomm partnered with Swedish airline Golden Air in 1999 until Finncomm obtained its own certificate in 2003. The original Golden Air fleet consisted of seven Saab 340s and one Saab 2000.[5] Under its own AOC, Finncomm started up flights between Helsinki and Stuttgart with one Embraer ERJ-145, leased from Swiss International Airlines. Later, flights to Düsseldorf and Oslo were started with a second aircraft of the same type. With the arrival of ATR 42s in November 2005, the Saab fleet, inherited from Golden Air, could be retired. What could have been a competitor for Finnair soon became an ally, when Finncomm started feeding passengers for Finnair's international route network. Finnair even agreed to offer additional training to Finncomm pilots on ATR aircraft, required by the Civil Aviation Administration. This organisation had imposed exceptional weather restrictions on the flight operations of the company's ATR aircraft because of Finnish weather conditions.[6] In September 2010, Finnair and Finncomm announced that Finnair would take a 20 per cent participation in Finncomm. At the same time, Finnair also acquired the entire Finncomm ATR fleet. Both airlines further made it clear it was the intention to find, in addition to Finnair, external investors in Finncomm.[7] The Finncomm Group then decided to sell the company to a joint venture between Flybe and Finnair for US$35m (£26m).[8] On 20 October 2011, following the acquisition by Flybe and Finnair, the jointly owned regional carrier became known as Nordic Regional Airlines; on that day, the airline also began operations. In March 2015, Flybe sold its 60 per cent participation to Finnair, which in turn sold the shares to Danish Air Transport.[9]

When Finnair celebrated its 75th anniversary in 1998, demand had increased again in all sectors, as the effects of the economic crisis in the early 1990s seemed contained. Passenger growth boomed and

Finnair carried nearly four million passengers in 1998. At that time, the government of Finland owned 59.80 per cent of the Finnair shares. The same year, Antti Potila retired as president of the airline. Of course, Helsinki remained the major hub for Finnair (good for 70 per cent of its turnover), but operations via the Swedish hub were also of interest, like the Helsinki–Stockholm–Manchester route.

The McDonnell Douglas MD-11 joined the fleet in the early 1990s. (Jozef Mols)

The new MD-11 became a logo-jet, promoting the Santa Claus Village in Rovaniemi. (Kenzo Ugawa)

Other aircraft in the fleet, like this MD-82, also carried promotion for Santa Claus Village. (Finnair)

Finnair brought Santa Claus to many airports arround the globe. (Finnair)

Above: Rovaniemi Airport, the gateway to Santa Claus village and Finland's arctic. (Visit Rovaniemi)

Left: Karair added ATR equipment to its fleet, which was used on Finnair's domestic network. (Jozef Mols)

Finnair decided to lease several Boeing 757s. (Tono Ayala)

Above: Leased 757-200s were used on charter flights to holiday destinations. (Ken Fielding/ Wikimedia Commons Licence)

Right: This 757-200 was leased by Finnair on one-year leases in 1998 and 2007 to complement its holiday charter fleet. (Raymond Zammit)

Below: As demand for cargo transportation increased, Finnair leased this Air Atlantic Iceland 737-200 in 1989. (Ken Fielding/ Wikimedia Commons Licence)

Finncomm offered feeder services for Finnair using a fleet of ATR 72 aircraft, seen here at Tallinn Airport. (Calflier 001/ Wikimedia Commons Licence)

Finncomm used both ATR 42 and ATR 72 aircraft on domestic feeder services for Finnair. (Kim Kujala/Wikimedia Commons Licence)

Chapter 6

Preparing for the New Millennium

Just like other airlines around the world, Finnair had to prepare for the upcoming new millennium and the challenges that would go with it. This burden would mainly rest on the shoulders of Keljo Suila, who took over as the new chief executive officer and president on 1 January 1999, when his predecessor, Antti Potila, retired. The last year of Potila's management had not been without problems. Although the year had started very well, growth tailed off during the second half, and the financial year ended with a difficult emergency situation, brought on by the strike of Civil Aviation Administration air traffic controllers.[1]

Finnair's profitability fell, while operating costs rose far faster than revenues. Operating costs were pushed up by expensive collective labour agreements and extra operational expenses. These were caused by a major increase in capacity and the switch to new Airbus aircraft and technology, which tied up an exceptional amount of resources for training. Whereas group financial performance was regarded as satisfactory, the downward trend in profitability was worrying. In Europe, the already prolonged growth in the volume of international air traffic had continued. Passenger numbers for the AEA (Association of European Airlines) had shown an increase of on average 6.5 per cent. During 1998, Finnair had exceeded this average until the strike, which began in February 1999 and lasted for six weeks, restricted traffic. All flights to Tallinn had to be closed. At the same time, a new partnership between SAS and Maersk, working in conjunction with Estonian Air, made it hard to for Finnair to build connections between Estonia and the rest of the world via its main hub in Helsinki. The industry, in general, was characterised by a serious decline in punctuality and an erosion of yield, shown by the fall in average revenues per passenger. The combined earnings of the AEA airlines had fallen by 20 per cent in 1998. The deterioration in air navigation services can be seen from the AEA's punctuality figures, which show an enormous increase in delays of about 40 per cent, compared with 1997.[2]

The globalisation of the customer base and the liberalisation and stiffening of competition gave added incentive to airlines to move towards closer and more extensive cooperation. Finnair decided, therefore, to join the oneworld Alliance in December 1999. Strong economic growth had fuelled air traffic growth in western Europe and the US, which was reflected in Finnair's passenger numbers, which increased by 5 per cent in 1998. However, this growth was restricted by economic problems, mainly in the Far East and Russia. As a result, intercontinental scheduled traffic had continued to grow with passenger numbers increasing by an average of 3.9 per cent over the previous year and the passenger load factor increasing from 73.8 per cent in 1997 to 74.9 per cent in 1998. On the other hand, Asian economies were unfavourable, which was reflected on all Finnair's Far East routes. The only route on which holiday passengers made up for the shortfall in other kinds of travel was Helsinki–Bangkok. Overall, the Atlantic routes maintained their passenger numbers at the previous year's level, although both the downturn in the Russian economy and the Balkan crisis, which occasionally affected Russian travelling habits, led to a clear decline in passenger volumes between Russia and the US, a market of which Finnair had a share of about 15 per cent.[3]

Other challenges remained. In the beginning of 1999, 11 European countries (Austria, Belgium, Finland, France, Germany, Ireland, Italy, Luxembourg, the Netherlands, Portugal and Spain) formed the single currency European Monetary Union. This meant that they were committed to adopting the euro as their common currency, to which the currencies of the member states were tied at a fixed rate. As the transition to the euro would take place in stages, Finnair had to draw up its own timetable by which the airline would move over to the euro. Preparation for the transition of bookkeeping, pricing, ticketing and more, of course, caused added costs. The abolition of tax-free sales on intra-European flights would leave a major dent in Finnair's earnings. The rise in fuel prices raised operating costs. As a result, Finnair decided to rationalise its route network by eliminating unprofitable routes.

The 'second home' of Finnair in Stockholm contributed to Finnair's profitability, although this route had also been affected by the air traffic controllers' strike. As Finnair had developed its Stockholm hub, from which the airline flew to 16 European cities, research showed that the Finnish carrier was almost as well known in Stockholm as SAS. This high profile was enhanced by Finnair's status as an official partner for Stockholm in its year as Cultural City of Europe in 1998. In turn, SAS bought Air Botnia, which operated low volume domestic routes. Before the takeover, Air Botnia's market share of Finnish traffic was about 3.7 per cent and remained below 4 per cent at the end of 1998.

In addition to its scheduled routes, Finnair also operated a fleet of aircraft dedicated only to leisure traffic. Most of the clients were Finnish package tour organisers who annually bought up almost the entire leisure fleet capacity. The risk of selling seats was taken on by the tour operators. Air traffic results from these leisure operations had increased strongly in previous years. In 1998, they went up by 12 per cent compared to the previous year and amounted to some FIM 1.2bn (£171m). The biggest clients of such flights were the Finnair subsidiaries, Suntours and Finntours, which together accounted for almost two thirds of the entire business. The operators used exclusively Finnair aircraft. Other clients were Fritidsresor and Hassen Matkat, which were part of the Thomson Group, and Tjäreborg and Spies, which belonged to the Airtours Group. Finnair's leisure department operated four Boeing 757s and two MD-83 aircraft during 1998, in addition to an MD-80, which was used for leisure flights at weekends. A further two MD-11s were used for winter traffic. During 1998, Finnair had flown 750,000 passengers on leisure flights to overseas destinations. The most popular places were in the Canary Islands. As Thomson and Airtours were planning to start flying from Finland to Spain with their own fleet, Finnair's market share would subsequently drop to 70–75 per cent. Therefore, Finnair was planning to transfer the MD-80 aircraft, used for leisure travel, to scheduled routes.

Cargo operations would also undergo changes prior to the new millennium. Finnair hauled two thirds of Finland's international air cargo. Whereas economic problems in Russia and Asia had a negative effect on cargo operations, the strong American dollar led to dramatically increased demand on North Atlantic routes as European firms increasingly directed their sales towards the US. The deregulation of aviation in Europe had opened up new opportunities in route planning and possibilities for expanding freight operations to cover the entire EU area. The Baltic states were expected to be part of a further expansion of the EU, increasing demand for air cargo as road links in those countries were rather poor. As Finnair cancelled its cargo route to Singapore, dedicated aircraft could be transferred to the Finland–US route. Finnair was operating a dedicated cargo fleet of one leased Airbus A300, two leased Boeing 727s and a single 747. Besides, cargo was also carried on all of the airline's regular flights. When the airline decided to buy Airbus A320s, this brought considerable benefits. Only containers would be used on the new aircraft, which would considerably speed up loading and unloading.

The first Airbus A321 went into service in February 1999. It was the first of 12 aircraft of this family (with options for an additional 24 aircraft). The first two aircraft were purchased for cash, whereas the other would be leased. It was the intention to replace the entire fleet of 37 DC-9s and MD-80s. The 178-seat A321 provided about 20 per cent more capacity than the largest of the MD-80s and would go into service on the most crowded European and domestic routes.

In 1999, Finnair started to enjoy the benefits of its membership of the oneworld Alliance. The airline estimated the increase in sales as a result of the membership amounted to some €24m (£20.5m). The alliance also brought savings on ground service costs, joint operational facilities, common purchasing and joint marketing campaigns. As a total result, all effects of the partnership taken together added some €69m (£58.8m) to Finnair's sales.[4] Joining a strong global alliance (including Aer Lingus, American Airlines, British Airways, Cathay Pacific, Iberia, LanChile and Qantas) enabled Finnair's customers to benefit from a global network consisting of close to 600 destinations and access to 350 common lounges.

On 27 September 1999, an Airbus A319 (the smallest aircraft of the Airbus family) entered commercial service. Prior to this introduction, the airline had already installed a new A320 simulator for its training centre. Overall, one can say that Finnair was well-prepared to enter the new millennium.

Right: **Airbus A321-200 OH-LZB – seen here at Brussels International Airport – was one of the first Airbus aircraft to be delivered to Finnair in November 1999. (Jozef Mols)**

Below: **This A319-100 entered Finnair's fleet in August 2000 and was leased via Finnair Aircraft Finance. (Jozef Mols)**

Finnair obtained the A319, A320 (like the one pictured here) and A321 aircraft. (Jozef Mols)

Above: When Finnair joined the oneworld Alliance, some of its new Airbus aircraft got the oneworld logo. (Valentin Hintikka/Wikimedia Commons Licence)

Left: Some of the new Airbus aircraft also received the Santa Claus paint scheme, like this A321 with sharklets. (Finnair).

OFFICIAL AIRLINE OF SANTA CLAUS

Right: Finnair's Santa Claus logo. (Finnair)

Below: The Santa Claus livery was widely used to promote travel to Rovaniemi. (Finnair)

Chapter 7

Problems Ahead

innair might have taken all measures necessary to enter the new millennium, but the airline could not predict the crisis ahead when the aviation world entered a new century. In 1999, the horizon still looked bright. The IATA predicted a global average annual growth estimate for all scheduled air traffic between 1999 and 2003 of some 3.8 per cent. For the period 2004–13, the organisation even predicted a growth rate for international scheduled travel of no less than 5.7 per cent per year.[1] Several factors were taken into account when these predictions were made. The air traffic deregulation process which began in 1987 in the EU/EEA area was brought to its end, while air transport within the member states was liberalised on 1 April 1997. Negotiations for the inclusion of ten Central and Eastern European countries in the 'third EU air transport package' were well underway, and when completed, this would lead to an expansion of deregulated European air traffic. Across the Atlantic, talks were going on about the creation of a Transatlantic Common Aviation Area (TCAA). However, it was more difficult to reach consensus on common rules between the continents than it was between European countries. Nevertheless, expectations were that such an agreement between the EU and the US would be signed in the next few years, thus promoting transatlantic air services.

The technical departments of Finnair performed well, as the airline was able to offer tailored services to both the parent airline and client airlines. About 60 per cent of the earnings from outside clients derived from contracts lasting many years. The biggest growth was experienced with the maintenance of the MD-11 aircraft, whereas servicing of customer's MD-80s was declining.

Although several factors seemed to be promising, Finnair's operational result was weakened. Profitability for the entire aviation industry had continued to weaken as airlines had increased their capacity and costs continued to rise at the same time. This resulted in fierce competition, pushing ticket prices downward. Finnair managed to preserve its 57 per cent market share in the home-market. However, the load factor dropped by 3.4 percentage points which, combined with the rise in fuel costs, reduced profitability. Fortunately for Finnair, the powerful upturn in the Finnish economy had a positive effect on demand for Finnair's business class travel. This increased demand was extremely strong on the European, North Atlantic and Far Eastern traffic. Demand for international business class travel surged by nearly 12.9 per cent, compared to the growth in demand for tourist class, which was only 3.5 per cent. The introduction of the airline's new Airbus A320 family of aircraft increased supply on core European routes. This new fleet formed the backbone of the fleet overhaul. In 2000, the airline placed a further order for six A320 type aircraft to be delivered between February 2002 and February 2003. At the same time, the airline sold six of its MD-80 aircraft, three of which were leased back for the company's own use while it awaited the arrival of the ordered A320s.

In response to the deregulation of European air traffic and the opening up of former Soviet-satellite states like the Baltic countries, Finnair started up the process to establish an Estonian airline and to acquire a licence for air traffic operations.[2,3] This application process was expected to lead to a positive result in January–February 2001. The aim of the company was to act as a significant airline operator in the Baltic area and between Estonia and Finland. Of course, in the future, the airline could also operate in the EU and in Scandinavia. Finnair took a 49 per cent participation in the new airline, while Aero Holding obtained 51 per cent of the shares. In a transition period, Finnair would supply the necessary ATR 72 aircraft, as well as the training of Estonian pilots. The new airline was called 'Aero Airlines AS', and this name harkens back to Finnair's first incarnation as Aero Oy back in 1923. The new Estonian carrier would operate all its flights under the Finnair designation code AY. The airline started up its operations in March 2002 within the Baltic region but had to scale down operations during 2007 because of financial issues and, finally, flew its last flight on 6 January 2008. All its former routes were taken over by Flybe and Finnair.

Finnair obviously noticed the powerful growth potential in Asia as a result of the continent's economic growth and resulting increased business travel. Therefore, Finnair increased the number of weekly flights to the most popular destinations of Beijing, Bangkok and Singapore and stopped its low-profit routes to Osaka, Toronto and San Francisco. As a result of this route overhaul, and more effective use being made of crews and aircraft, utilisation rates had risen and unit costs had fallen. Demand for cargo transportation had significantly increased, with annual growth rates of on average 6 per cent, and Finnair accounted for about 58 per cent of the Finnish air freight market. Cargo transportation within Europe had slowed down because of internal price competition among other forms of transport. Though, demand for air cargo from Scandinavian countries to the US was expected to increase. In accordance with the Finnair group's strategy of business development, the cargo division's activities were reorganised, and its operations would be restructured into a separate (subsidiary) company in 2001, under the name of Finnair Cargo Oy.

The leisure market showed some noticeable changes as well. Economic growth along with a greater appreciation of leisure time had a positive effect for holiday travel, but increases in fuel prices and the strengthening of the dollar had a negative effect on profitability for airlines in Europe. Concentration in the package tour sector continued within Europe. As a result, the package tour companies reduced their supply for the Finnish market and cut out sales of unprofitable last-minute flights. Thanks to this evolution, Finnair could increase its market share in the leisure market by more than 10 per cent to about 90 per cent. Leisure flights to some 60 destinations were mainly carried out by leased Boeing 757 aircraft.

As Finnair was well-known for the quality of its inflight meals, the airline delivered its services to several airlines. Catering services accounted for about 14 per cent of outside sales. The catering unit offered jobs to some 944 people in 2001. As a result of its success, Finnair Catering was made into a company and an independent business unit.

Of course, 2001 was also a year of downturn in Finnair's profitability when, because of the weakening of the international economy, passenger numbers dropped. The most significant change in demand occurred in business class travel, where the trend was negative from March 2001 onwards. Owing to the economic downturn, cargo transportation also decreased. Finnair Cargo had already reduced the freight capacity it hired from outside the group. One of the two weekly Boeing 747 cargo flights between Finland, Sweden and the US was discontinued. At the same time, Finnair changed its cargo partner from Polar Air Cargo to Evergreen International Airlines. In addition, internal European cargo routes were combined. On the other hand, as the Asian economy was still growing, it was decided to open a new route to Hong Kong in February 2002, as well as to increase the frequency of flights to China.

When, on 11 September, a terrorist attack took place in the US, the airline industry as a whole fell into one of its worst crises. Between September and December 2001, international traffic by European airlines fell by 17.6 per cent compared with the year before. The financial result for the industry for the year 2001 was a record low and certain airlines, already weakened by financial trends, could no longer survive the difficulties of the fall. Not only scheduled traffic, but also the leisure department, was hit by the attacks in New York. Demand for holiday tickets was significantly lower than that of a year earlier in the aftermath of the 9/11 attacks. This sharp drop in demand would lead to a reorganisation of the leisure traffic and the destinations served. The 9/11 attacks also resulted in new security measures that affected operational activities, flying costs and unit revenues. Owing to the severe collapse in demand for North Atlantic travel, Finnair conveniently transferred capacity from the New York route to the

Bangkok route. American Airlines, the oneworld Alliance airline that suffered in the 9/11 attacks, cut back its route network, thereby reducing the number of Finnair and American Airlines joint codeshare flights. Other airlines also cut back their operations. Air France, which used to fly between Paris and Helsinki, terminated these operations shortly after the attacks. Finnair and Air France subsequently agreed on codeshare operations whereby Finnair started flying to Paris four times a day, and Air France bought a quota of seats from Finnair's capacity, thus reducing Finnair's risk. Cooperation with Swissair and Sabena was cut off when these companies ceased flying because of financial difficulties. The Finnair group results for the financial year 2001, after financial items and excluding capital gains, showed a loss of €12.7m (£10.8m). Turnover had fallen by 1.6 per cent.[4]

Above: Finnair participated in the start-up of a new Estonian airline. (Andreas Hoppe/Wikimedia Commons Licence)

Left: Santa Claus did not forget the people in the cargo division. (Finnair)

Finnair operates a modern cargo centre at Helsinki airport. (Finnair)

Cargo, mainly to Asia and the US, contributes to Finnair's financial results. (Finnair)

Finnair's cargo department operates the most modern equipment. (Finnair)

Finnair's cargo department became an independent business unit at the beginning of the new century. (Finnair)

Finnair's catering department produces meals for its parent airline, but also for other airlines that fly to Finland. (Finnair).

Right: Top chef Rika Maezawa prepared Japanese meals for Finnair. (Finnair)

Below: A three-course meal in business class. (Finnair)

Chapter 8

Slow Recovery

In the introduction to the 2002 annual report, Finnair's CEO Keijo Suila stated that, in his opinion, the difficult period that started just after the beginning of the 21st century could continue for longer than expected.[1] The uncertainty and terrorist threats that overshadowed the global political outlook were reflected in the economy, and, of course, in air traffic. It seemed as if all airlines were expecting economic activity to contract, and travel would decline. The gravity of the situation was illustrated by figures that would have sounded unbelievable a few years earlier. Globally, on average, airlines had recorded more losses during the past two years than the total profits they made during the previous 45 years. However, the crisis also provided some advantages. Overcapacity in the airline industry would probably evaporate as weaker companies went bankrupt. Nevertheless, price competition remained strong in 2002, as companies that had suffered from the drop in business volume the previous years tried to recuperate some of their losses by attracting more passengers. As prices for aircraft dropped because of cancelled orders and bankruptcies, the threshold for newcomers had been lowered, so Finnair had to face increased competition from new market entrants. Notwithstanding all these challenges, Finnair managed to publish satisfying year end results. Its nearly debt-free status and a strong cash flow made it possible to withstand the knocks better than many competitors. Finnair could plan ahead, instead of depleting resources in a struggle for survival. The Asian market had remained very profitable despite the problems of the past years. In 2001, this market segment had grown by 17 per cent, and, in 2002, the growth rate even increased to 38 per cent. Therefore, the airline decided to further augment its Asian services by adding one MD-11 aircraft. During the 2001/02 winter, all four MD-11 aircraft had been overhauled to give them new identical cabins. With new flights to Osaka, Hong Kong and Shanghai and an increased number of flights to Beijing, the airline was strengthening its market position in the fastest growing market area for air transport. The flights to Bangkok – a major destination for leisure travel – were increased from four to seven a week. On the other hand, leisure flights to the Caribbean were discontinued due to low demand, but Fortaleza in Brazil was added to the leisure route map. One MD-11, previously used for leisure flights, was returned to the scheduled traffic department and replaced by two Boeing 757s, bringing the total number of this type to seven. In 2002, Finnair transported a total of 7,037,000 passengers (compared to 7,537,000 in 2001) and, thanks to capacity reductions, the overall load factor increased from 56.8 per cent in 2001 to 57.8 per cent a year later. These results were obtained with a fleet of 59 aircraft, of which 37 were owned and 22 leased.

Not all of Finnair's hopes for the future materialised. The recovery of demand that had begun after 2001 came to a halt in the summer of 2002. Overcapacity – although decreased – was not removed to the extent required by changes in demand. In 2002, Air Finland entered the Finnish market from its home base in Helsinki-Vantaa. The airline, which operated with a fleet of Boeing 757s, competed with Finnair's leisure department by flying passengers to holiday destinations in the Mediterranean and the Canary Islands. In 2007, 55 per cent of the shares would, however, be sold to Berling Capital Group, and, in June 2012, the airline had to suspend operations due to financial problems. In 2002, Flying Finn was incorporated with €1.7m (£1.5m) capital, starting up services in March 2003. Its cheap air fares resulted from e-tickets that were sold through the internet and phone. There were also no free meals during the flights and cancellation policies were restrictive. The start of the airline was promising, as passengers who used to use buses and trains now bought cheap airline tickets.[2] The airline operated a fleet of two MD-83 aircraft, which originated from Finnair and were leased from a financial group in the Cayman Islands. Its flight captains had also been employed earlier by Finnair. Flying Finn ceased operations in 2004 because of financial problems, leaving 20,000 passengers stranded.[3]

To aggravate Finnair's market outlook, the war in Iraq and the SARS epidemic contributed to a collapse in demand for air travel. When the epidemic receded at the end of 2003, capacity on Asian routes could be restored as demand recovered. Meanwhile, capacity had been adjusted according to the contracting demand. As sensible alternatives were sought for freed capacity, it was decided to open a route to Miami. In the third quarter of 2003, when the SARS epidemic receded, the proportion of passengers and cargo revenue coming from Asian traffic exceeded revenue from domestic flights for the first time in Finnair's history. In three years, China traffic had grown from two Beijing flights per week to 16 return flights per week to three destinations in China. Finnair offered the fastest connections between Far Eastern destinations and dozens of European cities.

As Finnair was also planning a growth strategy for the Scandinavian market, the airline acquired an 85 per cent shareholding in the Swedish carrier Nordic Airlink, which had a light-weight cost-structure and a flexible operating culture. For Finnair, Nordic Airlink was a strong opening into a new market with an initial small investment. It was Finnair's intention to grow Nordic Airlink into the Nordic countries' leading budget carrier. Nordic Airlink, which had its operating licence revoked in 2000 due to financial reasons, was rebranded as FlyNordic when Finnair took over the operation.[4] In its first year of operations under Finnair ownership, FlyNordic carried 725,000 passengers. In April 2007, Norwegian Air Shuttle announced that it had bought all FlyNordic shares from Finnair. As a result of the transaction, Finnair became owner of five percent of Norwegian Air Shuttle. On 14 March 2008, Norwegian Air Shuttle announced that FlyNordic would be re-branded as Norwegian.

Initiatives within the European Union were also a cause of concern. Any airline, domiciliated in the EU, can operate freely within the entire and expanded EU. Like other European countries, Finland was accustomed to negotiating bilateral operating agreements with countries outside the EU. In future, however, regulation at the EU level would bring the negotiation of aviation agreements between countries, both inside and outside the EU, under the jurisdiction of the European Commission. As a negotiating party, the EU is stronger than an individual country and thus can strengthen the position of European airlines when negotiating operating rights. In some cases, however, this might have an adverse impact on Finnair and might even weaken the airline's competitive position in the relation to other European airlines. In the past, Finnair had enjoyed outstanding agreements with Russia and many Far Eastern countries. If – through the negotiations of the EU – other European airlines might obtain the same conditions for their operations to Russia and Asia, Finnair would lose its competitive advantage.[5]

Notwithstanding adverse market conditions, Finnair carried more than 8 million passengers in 2004 (compared to 6,849,000 the year before): the first time in Finnair's history. Though, once again, the year had not been without trouble. The aftermath of the earthquake and tsunami in Asia forced the airline to act. Finnair employees were stretched to their limits as the evacuation was greatly supported by its tour guides and other volunteers in the devastated areas. Thousands of Finns had to be evacuated from the areas affected.

By the end of 2004, Finnair's five-year programme to acquire 29 Airbus A320 series aircraft was completed. In the meantime, the airline had also decided to acquire 12 Embraer E-170 jets. These would replace the remaining MD-80 and ATR 72 aircraft. Despite these investments, the airline remained nearly debt-free. Air travel had returned to a growth track after years of falling demand, but stiffening competition still pushed ticket prices down. The price for fuel had also increased, and the additional fuel bill for 2004 was €55m (£46.8m), despite the implementation of a price hedging policy. Aviation fuel accounted for 12 per cent of Finnair's costs. Fortunately, Asian traffic grew in 2004 by more than 40 per cent. As a result, the flight frequency to Osaka and Shanghai was increased to five return flights per week. Finnair also announced it would open a new route to Guangzhou on the Pearl River Delta in China in September 2005. On the transatlantic route, however, the only year-round destination was limited to New York. In the Baltic region, Finnair's subsidiary – the Estonian airline Aero – was doing well beyond expectations. Finnair, therefore, decided to transfer its entire turboprop traffic to Aero, which operated its routes with eight ATR 72 aircraft. In Finland, Aero's network covered the south of the country. In addition to the Helsinki–Tallinn route, Aero operated between Helsinki and Riga, Latvia, and to Vilnius, Lithuania, as well as, in the summer, to Kuressare on the Estonian island of Saaremaa.

In 2005, Keijo Suila retired as CEO of Finnair and was replaced by Jukka Hianon. At that time, the airline had over 9,000 employees and operated a fleet of 70 aircraft, including the fleets of Aero and FlyNordic. The passenger load factor had increased to 73 per cent after the bleak crisis years between 2001 and 2004. By the end of 2005, the airline announced that it would upgrade its long-haul fleet by 2021. The MD-11s, which had served the company well, would gradually be replaced by three Airbus A340 and nine A350 wide-bodied aircraft, the first of which would join the fleet in 2006. This change in equipment would allow the airline to save on fuel costs. On a typical Helsinki–Guangzhou flight, the MD-11 consumed 87 tonnes of fuel, which cost €47,850 (£40,725m). The A350 that Finnair ordered in 2005 would consume a third less fuel. The acquisition of the Airbus aircraft represented the biggest fleet modernisation in Finnair's history and clearly reflected Finnair's confidence and commitment to its Asian growth strategy.[6]

In the Baltic region, FlyNordic grew in line with expectations, and the company carried nearly 1.2 million passengers. The price trend in the Swedish market, however, was weaker than expected and fuel costs had increased, so FlyNordic's results remained in the red.

In 2002, Air Finland entered the leisure market and became an important competitor for Finnair. (Maarten Visser/ Wikimedia Commons Licence)

Right: Just like Finnair, Air Finland used Boeing 757s for its leisure flights. (Tony Brierton/Wikimedia Commons Licence)

Below: Low-cost carrier Flying Finn started competing with Finnair by providing cheap airline tickets for mainly domestic destinations. (Pertti Sipilä/Wikimedia Commons Licence)

Finnair obtained an 85 per cent shareholding in Nordic Airlink. (Aero Icarus/Wikimedia Commons Licence)

Above: When Finnair took over Nordic Airlink, the airline was rebranded as FlyNordic. (Aero Icarus/ Wikimedia Commons Licence)

Left: Finnair decided to buy a series of Embraer ERJ-170 jets. (Wikimedia Commons Licence)

Below: The ERJ-170 replaced some older aircraft types on mainly domestic and regional routes. (Aero Icarus/Wikimedia Commons Licence)

Chapter 9
Restructuring

Previous years had been characterised by a very slow growth after the decline in air traffic, and Finnair recognised the need to re-organise some of its operations. For the airline, international scheduled passenger traffic (which is its main business area) had been shaped by growing Asian traffic, which in turn influenced European routes. In 2006, Asian traffic had risen by nearly 30 per cent, whereas Finnair's total scheduled traffic had grown by some 13 per cent.[1]

Therefore, in the second quarter of 2006, a restructuring programme was initiated with the aim of finding €80m (£68m) of annual savings, starting in 2008. Over €15m (£12.7m) in non-recurring expenses for restructuring were earmarked for reduction in the second quarter, including a €10m (£8.5m) cut in personnel and an impairment of more than €5m (£4.3m) on Finnair Technical Services' inventories.[2] In a statutory employer-employee procedure, a reduction of 670 jobs by the end of 2007 was agreed. Most of the reductions would take place at the Technical Services department, as well as in administration. Negotiations were conducted with flight personnel to develop terms and conditions of employment to better correspond with Finnair's actual traffic structure. However, Finnair's goal of hiring 500 new employees for cabin work under the national collective employment agreement led to a dispute with the Finnish Flight Attendants' Association (SLSY), which organised a two-day strike at the end of October, resulting in a loss of some €10m (£8.5m). In negotiations and conciliation held after the strike, an agreement was reached for more flexible conditions of employment and, among other things, the establishment of a group that would focus on long-haul flights.[3] The negotiated deal should allow Finnair to save some €20m (£17m).

On 31 December 2006, Finnair had a fleet of 72 aircraft with an average age of 8.3 years. The use of the MD-80s was discontinued, and the aircraft was transferred to Finnair's Swedish subsidiary FlyNordic. The Estonian subsidiary Aero AS operated seven ATR 72s, but Finnair decided to sell four of them by the spring of 2007. The Embraer acquisition programme, which began in the summer of 2005, continued. In the meantime, the airline had obtained ten 76-seat Embraer E170s, as well as ten 100-seat Embraer E190s. For the growing Asian traffic, Finnair bought its first pre-owned Airbus A340 in July 2006. Furthermore, a seventh MD-11 had joined the fleet to provide cover during the winter when other MD-11s were overhauled. The lease agreements on three Boeing 757s were renewed on clearly more favourable conditions. It was also decided that, by 2007, these aircraft would be equipped with winglets to improve aerodynamics and thus reduce fuel consumption and emissions. This was an important step, as by the end of 2006, the EU announced a proposal for extending emissions trading to air transport around the turn of the decade. This emission trading would take into account the benefits produced for the fuel consumed. As it would only apply to airlines operating within the EU, however, the scheme would distort competition in the industry.

The restructuring – started in 2006 – soon showed positive results. Operating profit increased from €11m (£9.4m) in 2006 to €97m (£82.6m) the next year. Of course, traffic growth was also one of the contributing factors. In 2007, Asian traffic had grown again by 30 per cent from the previous years. Including leisure flights, Finnair could report a growth figure of 13 per cent. In order to make such increase in traffic possible, Finnair had added two more A340s to its fleet. This marked the beginning of the MD-11 replacement. Finnair planned to withdraw these aircraft from service in 2010 when their lease contracts would expire. To finance the fleet investment, Finnair launched a €248m (£211.3m) share issue directed at existing shareholders. Despite ever increasing fuel prices, unit costs for air traffic continued to fall. Key factors in this decline were more efficient fleet utilisation and an improvement in staff productivity. Air cargo traffic on Finnair's Asian flights grew because of an increase in capacity but average prices fell. This was particularly evident in the Scandinavian markets where new cargo routes to Sweden, created by Asian companies, resulted in overcapacity. As Asian traffic remained Finnair's 'bread and butter', the airline added Mumbai to its route network in June 2007, with five flights per week. Direct flights to the South Korean capital of Seoul were planned. A terminal expansion at Helsinki-Vantaa airport was planned to open in 2009, intended to service Asian traffic.

In spite of all efforts made by the company, results for 2008 remained weak. The air transport sector followed the general economic trend in a slightly more pronounced way. The early part of the year was a time of strong growth, but development of demand weakened towards the end of the year. Attempts to increase prices during the spring had a strongly adverse effect on the passenger load factors of Finnair's scheduled flights. A reduction of business travel and a shift to cheaper price classes rapidly undermined the average yield from flight tickets. A study for the full year revealed that revenue passenger kilometres on European airlines grew by a little more than 1 per cent, whereas capacity had increased by more than 3 per cent. This evolution had put pressure on ticket prices as competition increased. The arrival of new Airbus A330-300 equipment, to be used on Asian routes together with the A340s and the resulting withdrawal of the old MD-11s, was expected to result in lower costs in the next years. As the leasing agreements for five MD-11s would expire anyway, Finnair decided to sell the sixth MD-11 in the fleet to Aeroflot Cargo. To decrease its cost structure, Finnair proposed to cut wages and salaries by 5 per cent and to freeze previously agreed pay rises. However, this cost-cutting attempt was rejected by all employees of the group in December 2008. At the beginning of the consultation between the airline and the trade unions, Finnair threatened to cut jobs. One of the trade unions' objections was related to the fact that Asian flight attendants working the Finnair flights to Asia were paid considerably less than other Finnair employees.[4] The negotiation disputes were taken to a conciliator, but those propositions were also rejected by the trade unions, which questioned the impartiality of the conciliator.[5]

If 2008 was a troublesome year for Finnair, 2009 would even be worse, as major economic problems hit the entire aviation industry. One of the main reasons behind this was the evolution of the fuel price. At the beginning of 2008, oil (Brent Crude) started at $97 per barrel, but it hit $147 in July, threatening to add over $100bn to the industry fuel bill. By the end of the year, oil averaged out at $99 per barrel. The increase in fuel prices was in part explained by rising exploration and extraction costs. The real damage to airlines' expenses, however, was done by the speculation in oil that emerged somewhat later. Some analysts, like Goldman Sachs, were predicting additional increases to above $200 per barrel, stimulating further speculation amongst airlines.[6] By the end of the year, fuel prices had come down again, but this did not result in immediate relief for the airlines, as most of them had signed long-term contracts for oil as their management was afraid prices would further increase. As a result, many airlines paid more for their fuel than spot prices on the market after prices came down again.[7]

The other factor that led to larger than expected losses was the precipitous fall in traffic in key aviation markets. Air freight volumes, which are a timely indicator of international trade and economic activity, started to decline from the second quarter of 2008 onwards. By December 2008, air freight volumes had already collapsed more than 22 per cent below the level a year before.[8] The scale of this decline was unlike anything experienced before and reflected the unprecedented global drop in economic activity as a result of the 2008 worldwide banking crisis. As with air freight, passenger markets also began 2008 growing at a robust rate amid still solid economic growth worldwide, but once the banking crisis hit, passenger numbers declined. Business travel is highly sensitive to problems in the economy and fell fast. The wider impact of the September 2008 bankruptcy of New York-based Lehman Brothers in particular triggered a sharp fall in air travel by the financial sector, and especially on premium tickets. Later, the crisis in the financial sector spread to the manufacturing sector and particularly to export industries and finally to leisure travel, causing a worldwide problem for airlines.[9]

Of course, Finnair could not escape from these damaging factors, and it published a loss of €180m (£153.4m) in 2009. Turnover had declined sharply due to falls in both demand and ticket prices. Group turnover fell by 18.5 per cent. Profitability weakened as costs could not be adjusted quickly enough to match declining ticket and cargo price levels.[10] While demand had slowly recovered by the end of 2009, overcapacity in the sector put strong pressure on ticket prices and freight rates. To strengthen its balance sheet, Finnair issued a €120m (£102.2m) hybrid bond. The airline continued its efficiency programme to help the deteriorating profitability. A significant proportion of the planned efficiencies and cost savings would be achieved through collective employment and stabilisation agreements to be concluded with personnel, while some other savings would be found via temporary lay-offs and redundancies. During 2009, the Finnair group had an average number of 8,797 employees, which was 8.3 per cent fewer than a year before. A year before, strikes had already impacted Finnair's results, and it was feared this would happen again. Indeed, industrial action took place in ground handling operations when a partnership arrangement was reached with Barona and RTG Ground Handling in respect of baggage handling and loading operations. Finnair decided to sell these operations to this outside company. At the beginning of December 2009, around 500 employees who had been transferred to these employers held a four-day strike. Once again, a national conciliator was appointed in an attempt to resolve the dispute between the Finnish Aviation Union and the new staff service companies Barona and RTG Ground Handling. An agreement was finally reached by the end of January 2010.[11]

By the end of 2009, Finnair operated a fleet of ten Embraer E170s. (Jozef Mols collection)

Above: The E170 fleet was joined by some ten larger E190s. (Eric Salard/Wikimedia Commons Licence)

Left: The Embraer E190 was mainly used on European routes. (Arto Häkkilä/Wikimedia Commons Licence)

Below: By the end of the decade, Finnair introduced the Airbus A340 on its long-haul flights. (John Taggart/Wikimedia Commons Licence)

The A330-300 was also introduced on long-haul flights. (BriYYZ/Wikimedia Commons Licence)

The introduction of the A330-300 was another step in the cost-saving programme, introduced at Finnair in the first decade of the 21st century. (Raymond Zammit)

Chapter 10

The Moomins and Angry Birds™

Finnair said farewell to its last McDonnell Douglas MD-11 on 22 February 2010, when flight AY022 took off from Delhi for its final flight to Helsinki. The type had served Finnair for nearly 20 years, during which time it flew some 400,000 hours, landed more than 50,000 times and transported 14 million passengers. The type played a crucial role in Finnair becoming 'the fastest airline between Asia and Europe' by being a great workhorse on the Nordic routes to Asian destinations. Finnair had been the launch customer of the MD-11 and, as such, became the first airline to operate the type in December 1990.[1] Finnair had up to seven MD-11s at one time, which were replaced by Airbus A330s and A340s.

During its years in operation, the MD-11 had also served as billboard for Finnair, as well as for Finnish companies. Finnair MD-11 OH-LGB could be seen in a special Moomin livery scheme. The Moomins (Mumintrollen in Swedish or Muumit in Finnish) are the main characters in a series of books and comic strips by Swedish-speaking Finnish author Tove Jansson. Moomin merchandising became an important part of her income. Nobody could have predicted how popular Moomin porcelain mugs would become for example. Finnish ceramics company Arabia will not reveal exactly how many Moomin mugs have been sold, but admits the figure is in the millions. The most popular is the pink 'Love' mug, which has been in production since 1996. Some of the special editions have become collector's items, fetching prices of up to €6,000 (£5,100) at auctions. It is no wonder Finnair decided to catch the attention of the public by painting one of its MD-11s with the Moomin characters.[2] The Moomins are especially popular in Asia, and Finnair carried many eager passengers to the Moominworld theme park (Muumimaailma in Finnish) in Naantali, Finland, or the Moomin Museum in Tampere, Finland.

When the MD-11s were withdrawn from service, Finnair decided to paint one of its A340-300s with another special livery. The decision to drive awareness of the airline's new route to Singapore came at a time when the Finnish computer game developer Rovio Mobile launched a puzzle video game by the name of Angry Birds™. Over 12 million copies of the game were sold. In 2011 – after painting one of its aircraft with Angry Birds™ pictures – Finnair operated a special Angry Birds™-themed flight between Helsinki and Singapore. During the flight on 20 September 2011, Angry Birds™ fans and other passengers were able to participate in a competition on games consoles, distributed to passengers and specially programmed for this event. 'It's great to be involved in bringing Finnish innovation to Asia', said Jarkko Konttinen, Vice President for Global Brand and Marketing Communications at Finnair.[3] Upon arrival, the Asian Angry Birds™ Challenge was presented for Singaporean and international media in a press event, which discussed Angry Birds™ as a phenomenon bigger than just a mobile game.

While the MD-11 was withdrawn from passenger service, it was not the end of the aircraft for Finnair. In 2011, Nordic Global Airlines Ltd (NGA) was incorporated as a cargo airline. Main shareholders were Neff Capital Management LLC (20 per cent), Daken Capital Partners LLC (29 per cent) and the Mutual Pension Insurance Company Ilmarinen (11 per cent). Finnair had a 40 per cent share participation in the airline. Since its incorporation, NGA grew to fly main-deck cargo in four continents with a fleet of MD-11s (two of which once served in the Finnair fleet). Between 2011 and 2014, Finnair leased freighter capacity from NGA for its mainly Asian cargo traffic. As delivery of new A350s was delayed by the re-designing of the model at Airbus, Finnair considered this leasing as an interim solution. When the A350s eventually joined Finnair's fleet, cargo was carried in the cargo holds of these passenger aircraft, and services through NGA would be discontinued. However, overcapacity in the sector and depressed freight pricing forced NGA to cease operations in 2015.

Despite Moomins and Angry Birds™, Finnair had to solve more urgent problems. As IATA CEO Giovanni Bisignani put it in IATA's *Annual Report 2010*: 'Shocks and crises have exposed the weakness of the industry structure. The nearly $50 billion loss over the last decade is a blunt case for big change. Cautious optimism is returning. But challenges continue. We must rebuild the industry on a new and more resilient foundation.'[4] During 2009, airlines lost US$9.9bn, while passenger traffic fell 2.1 per cent and cargo dropped 9.8 per cent. Average yields tumbled 14 per cent and industry revenues fell 15 per cent.[5] The scale of the financial shock in 2009 came into focus with a comparison to the aftermath of the tragic events of September 2001. At that time, revenue fall was 'only' 7 per cent, nearly one third of the fall in 2009. Of course, Finnair was not hit as hard as other airlines, as the airline had concentrated its activities in the Nordic and Asian markets, whereas other airlines also had to cope with the effects of the Greek debt crisis, which affected customer behaviour in Europe. Nevertheless, in 2010, the airline saw its passenger numbers drop to 7,139,000 (compared to 7,433,000 in 2009 and even 8,792,000 in 2006). The year 2010 began in conditions of lower demand and price levels for passenger traffic than the previous year. Cargo demand, on the other hand, resumed growth in late 2009, which was reflected in improving cargo prices during spring 2010.[6] The upturn in cargo rates was highly concentrated in a few markets, especially in Asia, where the economic recovery had been strong. However, trade within Asia is fairly one-sided, with more being exported than imported. Together with a shortage of cargo capacity in Asia, this helped freight rates from Southeast Asia to Europe recover to pre-recession levels. By contrast, rates in the opposite direction had barely moved from their depressed levels.[7] The rapid recovery of the cargo market can be explained by a rapid post-recession growth, driven by the business inventory cycle. Air freight was the transport mode of choice when firms needed to restock at the start of the economic recovery. Though once inventory-to-sales ratios regained equilibrium by the middle of 2010, shippers no longer needed the time advantage provided by air freight, and sea transport began to regain market share.[8]

Structurally, Finnair progressed in line with the general development of the sector. The positive development in unit revenue in Finnair's scheduled traffic was stronger than the rest of the sector, owing to the structure of the sector. Indeed, business travel rose quickly in traffic between Europe and Asia. On the other hand, nearly all European traffic was affected by the ash cloud that followed the volcanic eruption of the Eyjafjallajökull in Iceland in April and May 2010. The aviation sector had to cancel about 100,000 flights because of flight restrictions over the course of a week. Of course, Finnair too suffered significant losses due to the traffic chaos. In addition, Finnair's traffic was disrupted by a ten-day long strike by cabin staff in December. Without the traffic disruptions experienced, Finnair's financial year might have been profitable.[9] Now, however, Finnair had to publish a loss of €5m (£4.25m) – a far better result than 2009 when the airline faced a €171m (£145.5m) loss – but still a loss nevertheless. As Finnair had implemented many efficiency measures the year before, these had helped production costs to rise more slowly compared to turnover. Personnel expenses fell more than production volume thanks to temporary lay-offs, redundancies and other measures. During 2010, the Finnair group offered jobs to 7,578 employees, which was 13.9 per cent less than the year before. Finnair's fleet had once again been modernised with the arrival of two new A330-300 aircraft in early 2010 and a third one more in the final quarter. The fleet was further supplemented by two A340-300s, after which Finnair had a long-haul fleet of 15 aircraft. As part of the harmonisation of its fleet structure, Finnair withdrew from service three Boeing 757-200s and ordered five new Airbus A321ER with wingtip sharklets. At the same time, the lease period for its four remaining 757s was extended.

Above: The Moomin MD-11 became an eye-catcher and promoted both Finnair and the illustrator who invented the Moomins. (Samuli Viikari)

Left: The two sides of the Moomin MD-11 each showed a different series of characters. (Contri/ Wikimedia Commons Licence)

Below: The Moomin MD-11 touching down at Helsinki-Vantaa Airport. (Antti Havukainen/Wikimedia Commons Licence)

Right: A Finnair stewardess with a Moomin character. (Finnair)

Below left: Angry Birds™ on the engine of an Airbus A340. (Jozef Mols collection)

Below right: Painting Angry Birds™ on a Finnair jet. (Jozef Mols collection)

The Angry Birds™ aircraft touching down. (Shimin Wikimedia/Commons Licence)

Chapter 11

Return to Profitability

The past few years had not been very successful for Finnair shareholders, as the airline had made losses, just like the rest of the airline industry. According to IATA, however, by March 2010, cargo and passenger traffic were within only 1 per cent of pre-recession highs, but yields were still 13 per cent down. A strong cyclical upturn in all regions (except Europe) gave hope for bottom line improvements.[1] The $9.9bn losses in 2009 for the whole sector turned into $18bn in profits in 2010. Against a worldwide capacity expansion of 5.2 per cent, demand increased by 10.3 per cent,[2] but the first quarter of 2011 reminded managers that the industry remained fragile. Demand was dampened by political unrest across the Middle East and North Africa, caused by the Arab Spring, and by the tragic earthquake and tsunami in Fukushima (Japan). Political uncertainty also drove oil prices to an average of $129 per barrel for the first months of 2011. Finnair admitted that all these facts weakened its results in 2011.[3]

As Finnair had a very strong market position in Asia – one of the fastest growing economies in the world – it is clear the airline wanted to focus on increasing Asian traffic in cooperation with a strong partner network. As Finnair's passengers continued their journey from Asia via Helsinki to other European destinations on Finnair's partners, a strong cooperation with Swissport – a leading ground service provider – began. To increase its presence in Asia, Finnair launched a new route to Singapore in 2011 and decided to add Chongqing to its route network a year later. Chongqing was the largest and fastest growing city in China, making it a significant destination for the implementation of Finnair's Asian strategy. Propelled by strong growth in Asia, Finnair's turnover increased by nearly 12 per cent in 2011 to reach €2,300m (£1,956m). Still, the airline had to publish a loss of nearly €60m (£51m) for the year 2011. As a result of the catastrophe in Japan, demand for tickets from Europe to Japan decreased significantly. The demand for flights between Japan and Europe, on the other hand, recovered more rapidly. About 70 per cent of passengers on Finnair flights between Japan and Europe were Japanese citizens. In the European market, Finnair decided to introduce new pricing categories for domestic and intra-Scandinavian flights. The purpose of the new price categories was to attract new customer segments in the market and make flying a more attractive alternative in regional traffic. In order to increase fleet productivity on regional routes, the capacity of the A320 fleet was being increased through new cabin configurations. In an effort to implement a comprehensive identity renewal, Finnair's cabin crew began to wear their new uniforms, designed by Ritva-Liisa Pohjalainen, in December. In addition to the uniforms, Finnair renewed the company logo and aircraft livery, as well as the look of the cabins.

A year later, Finnair's efforts resulted in a return to profitability. The airline published a profit of €44.9m (£38.2m). During 2012, the airline had managed to achieve a cost savings of nearly €100m (£85m), notwithstanding a new strike. In June 2012, technicians and clerical officers had gone on strike against outsourcing. The dispute was sparked by plans to shut down or scale back certain activities by Finnair's technical staff in a move expected to lead to the loss of 280 jobs. After two days of disruptions, Finnair took the trade unions to court. The Helsinki District Court granted an injunction to the company to end the action, and the strikers were forced to go back to work on 7 June under the threat of a fine of €2.8m (£2.38m). Many influential Finnish jurists and professors of law condemned the strike injunction as illegal, arguing that the court had no jurisdiction to intervene in the employees' fundamental right to take industrial action.[4] After a dramatic intervention by the National Labour Conciliator, negotiations continued between the trade unions and Finnair. The dispute was resolved on

14 June, when Finnair and the trade unions reached an agreement on support packages for technical and salaried staffs facing redundancy.

To further expand its Asian footprint, the airline announced it would open two new summer destinations: Xian in China and Hanoi in Vietnam. Through this, Finnair became the first European carrier to offer direct flights between Europe and Xian. However, other European carriers also started up new routes to Asia, thus increasing competition on Finnair's main routes. In the annual report for 2012, the CEO of Finnair announced that, overall, 2012 had been a gratifying year for Finnair, which had made a profit of €44.9m (£38.2m), despite an increase of the fuel bill by nearly €100m (£85m).[5]

In June 2013, Finnair proudly opened its new head office, known as House of Travel and Transportation (HOTT), on what used to be a car park right next to its previous head office on the grounds of Helsinki Airport. The construction of HOTT began in July 2011, and the previous office had been in use since 1994.[6] Also in 2013, Finnair took delivery of the first of its five sharklet-fitted extended-range Airbus A321 aircraft on order, becoming the launch customer for the A321ER, which were intended to replace the Boeing 757s.

By the end of 2012, Finnair announced it would start an inflight design collaboration with Finnish design house Marimekko. From spring 2013 onwards, all Finnair aircraft featured a 'Marimekko for Finnair' collection of textiles and tableware, incorporating Marimekko's classic patterns. Two of Finnair's long-haul aircraft also featured external livery based on Marimekko designs. An A340, featuring designer Maija Isola's iconic Unikko floral poppy print from 1964, started operating between Helsinki and Asia, followed by a second aircraft a few months later.[7] Although the Unikko poppy design was well received by the public, one Chinese journalist came up with an interesting question during the press presentation of the A340 in Beijing. 'Here in China, poppies are considered not only beautiful but also dangerous. Why did you decide to paint poppies on your plane?' he politely asked. Fortunately, the Finnair representatives could reply to the question by telling the story of the iconic print, which is important, but at the same time, the question highlighted the significance of understanding the local market and culture when starting up new routes. It would have been beneficial to know that the opium trade, carried out by British merchants in the 19th century, contributed to the fall of the Chinese Empire and that opium was acquired from ...poppies![8]

In 2013, Pekka Vauramo had taken over the helm as Finnair's CEO. In the first annual report he submitted in this position, he had to admit that in 2013, financially at least, the year did not live up to the expectations of the airline. Despite a slow growth of air traffic worldwide, Finnair's turnover had fallen by 2 per cent from 2012, totalling €2.4bn (£2.04bn). The main factor slowing down turnover growth was the fall in euro-denominated revenue because of the substantial depreciation of the Japanese yen. Asian traffic was good for nearly half of Finnair's passenger traffic and Japan was, at that time, Finnair's second largest market after Finland. In the second half of the year, the weaker-than-expected development of cargo and leisure traffic also contributed to the decrease in turnover for the full year. Leisure travel to Egypt had to be cancelled for the entire winter season because of unrest in the country. Once again, Finnair's balance sheet turned red, showing a loss of €4.8m (£4.08m).[9] Nevertheless, Finnair had to prepare for two significant waves of investment. In 2015, the airline would take delivery of the first of its new Airbus A350 long-haul aircraft, and, in the coming two years, the airline also had to look into the renewal of the European fleet to ensure future competitiveness and energy efficiency. Finnair continued to take advantage of the growing demand for traffic between Europe and Asia by providing the fastest connections between them thanks to Helsinki's strategic location, high-quality service and cost-efficient punctual operations.

When following this strategy, Finnair was taking care of megatrends and phenomena that had a strong impact on the future and consumer behaviour in the long term. The gradual shift in economic and political focus from the US and Europe to developing countries – and Asia in particular – was the strongest of the megatrends affecting the aviation industry. Asian companies were becoming globalised, and their significance in the world markets was growing. The Asian middle class was also growing. As a result, Asian travel was expected to further increase, and competition on Asian routes would intensify as Asian airlines – but also carriers from the Persian Gulf – would expand their operations. Non-Asian airlines would also have to increase their understanding of Asian culture and customers. In 2013, Finnair was already flying to 13 Asian megacities: Tokyo, Osaka, Nagoya, Seoul, Beijing, Shanghai, Chongqing, Xian, Hong Kong, Hanoi, Bangkok, Singapore and Delhi. With migration flows from rural areas to cities continuing at a accelerating speed, particularly in China, the number of cities with more than five million inhabitants would grow, thus creating new markets for air travel.

Another megatrend to be followed by Finnair was the dramatic digital communications revolution, which reshaped customer expectations every day. Paperless ticketing had already been the norm for Finnair, and the airline supported the goals of IATA's Fast Travel, an automation programme for commercial aviation covering check-in, baggage drop, document check, boarding, flight rebooking and baggage recovery. In 2013, Finnair was awarded 'Fast Travel Gold' status by IATA for introducing automated and digital mobile processes for all of these activities at Helsinki Airport and many outstations, reducing queues at airports. Social media determined the way in which customers – or potential customers – got information, interacted with each other and connected with brands. In many countries, people spend more time on Facebook than watching TV. Customers were already talking about Finnair in social media, whether the company actively engaged with them or not. This forced the airline to engage with customers directly on various social media in six languages: English, Finnish, Swedish, Chinese, Japanese and Korean. In March 2013, Finnair introduced an optional social check-in service whereby passengers' Facebook profiles can be linked with the seat map during the seat-selection process, enabling greater sociability on board for those wishing to provide their Facebook profiles. Of course, passengers can also travel 'incognito' as before, as, in this hyper-connected world, people might just be happy to disconnect for a while or at least for the duration of a flight. In order to guarantee perfect inflight service, all Finnair's Asian routes are served by at least three locally based cabin crew members able to provide service in the customers' native language.

In September 2013, Finnair entered into an agreement to sell and leaseback two new A321 Sharklet aircraft and, in December, signed memorandums of understanding on the sale and leaseback of three new A321 Sharklet aircraft, four Finnair-owned A330s and two new A350 aircraft. These arrangements were part of the fleet renewal programme, which involved replacing the 330 and 340 fleet with next generation 350s, the first of which was expected to be delivered in the second half of 2015.

Above left: In order to modernise its image, Finnair introduced new uniforms for cabin staff, designed by a Finnish designer. (Finnair)

Above right: Of course, the crew also received a new winter uniform. (Finnair)

Right: The crew proudly shows off their new uniforms in front of new Airbus A350. (Finnair)

Below: Finnair painted this A340 with the Marimekko Unikko design to promote the Finnish designer in Asia. (Masakatsu Ukon/Wikimedia Commons Licence)

Above left: The Marimekko A340 upon arrival. (Valentin Hintikka/Wikimedia Commons Licence)

Above right: The 'poppy' design by Marimekko was not immediately understood by all Chinese journalists. (Raymond Zamitt)

Chapter 12

The Arrival of the New Airbus A350 XWB

The year 2014 was mainly characterised by a substantial decrease in unit passenger and cargo traffic, particularly in the first half of the year. Further factors in the decline were the contraction of sales in the leisure market and the loss of external turnover, resulting from the restructuring of aviation services, such as the divestment of Finncatering and the airport shops of Finnair Travel Retail. As fuel prices continued to decrease however, Finnair's balance sheet remained strong, and the financial position remained good.[1] Cost-saving agreements with personnel and trade unions cleared the way for unobstructed operations in the years to come.

Finnair worked hard to further improve already outstanding services the airline provided to its passengers. On long haul flights, new full flat seats were introduced. Another upgrade was the introduction of the Economy Comfort package: a new offering in the front of the Economy Class cabin featuring at least four inches of extra legroom, comfortable headrests and high-quality headphones. Catering on European flights was renewed with the introduction of the Sky Bistro service. This new service offered a high-quality mix and match selection of warm meal options, bought on board or tailored in advance at finnair.com (pre-order meals). At Helsinki airport, Finnair lounges were renovated and expanded with more than 40 per cent more lounge capacity in the Schengen-area lounge and a new Premium Lounge annex in the non-Schengen area. New shower suites and a small play area for kids were also introduced. As a result of all its improvements, Finnair was named Northern Europe's Best Airline for the fifth consecutive year in SkyTrax's World Airline Awards, and this was despite a difficult cost reduction exercise.

A major challenge for the entire airline industry was the upcoming problem of climate change. Finnair had started to report on its environmental efforts. The Carbon Disclosure Project (CDP) awarded Finnair a position on the A-list: the CDP Climate Performance Leadership Index 2014 for actions to reduce carbon emissions and mitigate the business risks of climate change. Finnair was the only airline worldwide awarded this A-grade. Finnair's efforts in this area were also recognised in January 2015 when the airline became one of the first two airlines to be certified as a Stage 2 operator in the IATA Environmental Assessment programme. The system was designed to independently assess and improve an airline's environmental management. In September 2014, Finnair was the only airline to fly to New York for the UN Climate Summit, using a more environmentally friendly biofuel mixture that was partly manufactured from recycled cooking oil. Together with other partners, Finnair even started investigating the possibility of establishing a biofuel hub at Helsinki Airport.

Even with all the efforts made, the airline did not succeed in keeping its books in the green. The airline booked a full-year operational loss of €36.5m (£31m). Nevertheless, the airline began operations to a series of new Scandinavian destinations including Tromso in Norway and had increased winter flights to Finnish Lapland, in particular to Kittilä, Ivalo and Kuusamo, in order to increase connections between Asia and Lapland's leisure destinations, which are very popular in Asia. Finnair also had started up services to Kazan, Nizhny Novgorod and Samara in the Russian Federation, along with a new direct service to Miami.

The oneworld Alliance, which Finnair joined in 1999, completed a major expansion drive with new members like SriLankan Airlines, TAM Airlines and American Airlines' merger partner US

Airways. Finnair's customers could earn and redeem Finnair Plus Points while travelling to nearly 1,000 destinations around the globe in more than 150 countries. In April 2014, Finnair entered into a joint business with oneworld partners British Airways and Japan Airlines, offering expanded schedules and connections between Japan and Europe for its customers. US Airways' merger with American Airlines meant that it joined the Atlantic Joint Business (with Finnair, American Airlines, British Airways and Iberia) on traffic between the EU and North America, adding 28 transatlantic routes to the joint business.[2] Furthermore, as stated previously, Finnair's geographical position in Helsinki enabled long-haul flights to Asia to be operated as round trips within 24 hours. To support this, the airline ordered eight additional A350 aircraft by the end of the year. The airline indeed firmed up the eight Airbus A350XWB aircraft options in its 2006 A350 order. Delivery was planned to start in 2018. This decision increased Finnair's A350 order to 19. At the same time, it was planned to phase out its A340s by the end of 2017. As part of the A350 deal, Airbus agreed to acquire four A340-300 aircraft, which were owned by Finnair.[3] Nearly at the same time, it was announced that Finnair had signed a memorandum of understanding with GOAL German Operating Aircraft Leasing GmbH & Co.KG on the sale and leaseback of three Embraer E190 aircraft. The proceeds of the transaction would be used to finance Finnair's fleet investment in the coming years.[4]

Finnair Cargo remained the largest cargo carrier in the Nordic region, transporting more than 150,000 tonnes of freight and mail annually, mainly between Europe and Asia with cargo logistic hubs in Helsinki and Brussels. Brussels was an important key delivery hub for pharmaceuticals – a growth opportunity for Finnair – as European pharmaceuticals, such as vaccines and biotech medicines, became more in demand in China and other Asian countries.

Fortunately for Finnair, the financial tide turned a little bit in 2015, when the airline booked an operational result for the full year of €23.7m (£20.01m). The airline hit a new record by transporting more than ten million passengers that year. The fall in fuel prices that began a year earlier, continued. Nevertheless, its impact was not yet fully reflected in the airline's results because of a hedging policy. Finnair had signed several long-term contracts when fuel prices had increased, and had to continue honouring those contracts, despite the decrease in fuel prices. Furthermore, the appreciation of the dollar against the euro further diluted the advantage gained by airlines from the substantial decrease in the price of jet fuel. It also significantly increased other dollar-denominated costs. However, at the same time, several different income currencies appreciated against the euro, which had a positive effect on Finnair's results. The American dollar is the most significant currency when it comes to paying Finnair's expenses, but the Japanese yen and Chinese yuan are very significant income currencies for them as well.[5]

The arrival of the long-expected Airbus A350XWB was, of course, a great step forwards in the fleet renewal programme. Finnair became the first European operator and the third worldwide of the all-new Extra Wide Body airliner. The new aircraft was configured with 297 seats in a three-class layout with 46 seats in Business Class, 43 seats in Economy Comfort and 208 seats in Economy. The aircraft entered into long-haul service on the Helsinki–Shanghai route. As Finnair was hoping to double its Asia traffic by 2020 from the 2010 baseline, the acquisition programme of the A350 was the backbone of this strategy.[6] The new aircraft would also play a key role in Finnair's cargo strategy, providing up to 50 per cent more cargo capacity.

Finnair also decided to add seating capacity to its feeder fleet. According to the plan, a number of seats would be added to the Airbus narrow-body fleet without changing the leg space available to passengers. Instead, space efficiency was improved by modifying storage and technical space in the front and the rear of the aircraft. The layout changes would take two weeks per aircraft and would start in 2017.[7] Also to increase capacity on regional routes, two airberlin A321 aircraft began operating Finnair flights from Helsinki to some European destinations. Under the damp lease agreement, airberlin delivered the pilots whereas cabin crew came from Finnair.[8]

In order to finance the acquisition of the new A350s and expansion of the feeder fleet, Finnair needed some 'financial engineering' to secure the necessary funds. In December 2014, Finnair had concluded a sale and leaseback deal with Doric Asset Finance GmbH & Co for six ATR 72 aircraft, owned by Finnair but operated by a feeder airline Norra (Nordic Regional Airlines). Norra operated a fleet of 26 aircraft for Finnair on a contract flying basis. Of the aircraft in Norra's fleet, 13 were owned by Finnair and another 13 were leased. Finnair concluded another sale and leaseback with GECAS (GE Capital Aviation Services) of its first two A350 XWB aircraft on their delivery dates. In December 2015, Finnair signed another agreement with GECAS on the sale and leaseback of two more A350s to be delivered in 2016 and 2017.[9]

On 13 October 2015, Finnair issued a €200m (£170m) hybrid bond, which was significantly oversubscribed by eager investors. In December, the airline sold certain facilities at the Helsinki Airport to Finavia as part of the development of the infrastructure of the airport. The transactions included Finnair's cargo terminal, which was to be decommissioned in 2017, and an office building, which was jointly owned by Finnair and Finavia. The deal would allow Finavia to expand the airport terminal. To replace the hangar, Finnair purchased another hangar at another location on the airport.

Left: A Finnair A330 also received the Marimekko paint scheme. (Jozef Mols collection)

Below: The arrival of the Airbus A350 XWB was a giant step forward in Finnair's fleet renewal programme. (Gyrostat/Wikimedia Commons Licence)

Above: The new A350 XWBs were introduced on Asian routes. (Matsakatsu Ukon/ Wikimedia Commons Licence)

Right: The introduction of the A350 XWB drastically increased Finnair's cargo capacity. (Finnair)

Below left: Large volumes of cargo can be transported on passenger flights with the A350. (Finnair)

Below right: Loading cargo aboard an A350 XWB. (Finnair)

Above: The business class section aboard a Finnair A350 XWB. (Finnair)

Left: The economy class cabin aboard the new A350 XWB. (Finnair)

The Schengen lounge at Helsinki Airport was full redecorated. (Finnair)

Above: Fluctuating fuel prices remained a problem for airlines around the world. (Finnair)

Right: Finnair was well aware of the impact of flying on the climate change. (Finnair)

IN FACT, SMALL IS BEAUTIFUL. AND WE'RE CUTTING OUR CARBON EMISSIONS 50% BY 2050.

Chapter 13
Flying Along the Silk Road

When Finnair published its annual report for 2016, it could safely say that a spirit of enthusiasm had returned. After some difficult years, revenues increased by 3 per cent and the operating profit had more than doubled to €55m (£46.8). The most important decision of the year was to accelerate Finnair's growth. Initially, and while the airline was phasing out its Airbus A340 aircraft, it also intended to take out two A330 aircraft while taking delivery of the new A350s. Instead, the airline decided to keep all the A330s, which materially strengthened the long-haul fleet. The airline also obtained new A321s for the feeder traffic. Owing to this growth strategy, the airline also had to accelerate the recruitment of flight crews. In 2016, a total of 280 staff members joined the airline.[1] Besides, the airline decided to hire 70 software developers, project managers, service designers and other digital experts in 2017.

There is no doubt that Finnair's growth was only possible thanks to its strategic location on 'the new Silk Road' – the ancient trade route that once ran between China and the West during the days of the Roman Empire. In 2013, Chinese President Xi Jinping resurrected this trade route when he announced his country wanted to reopen channels of commerce between China and its neighbours in the West: most notably Central Asia, the Middle East and Europe. The aim of the US$900bn scheme, as China explained, is to kindle a 'new era of globalization', a golden age of commerce that would benefit all. Of course, reactions were rather mixed, as the rest of the world expressed suspicion about China's true geopolitical intentions. The strong incentive is that Trans-Eurasian trade could bolster poorer countries to the south of China, as well as boost global trade. Chinese regions were also expected to benefit, especially the less-developed border regions in the west of the country, such as Xinjiang.[2] Recognising the importance of this reopening and to support its own income, Finnair decided to add more frequent flights to Hong Kong and Tokyo and, hence, became the biggest European airline to Japan with 23 weekly flights to four Japanese cities. In 2016, Finnair announced its growth strategy aimed to double the Asian traffic by 2018, two years earlier than the previous target of 2020. In 2016, Finnair's market share in travel between European countries and Asia had reached 5.6 per cent. Aside from passenger traffic, Finnair's cargo operations also benefit from increased East–West trade. At both ends of the link, a fan-like network opens up through which the population centres of the Far East and Europe are reached flexibly and efficiently.

However, the new Silk Road has been a cause of concern to some. Russia has attempted to create a Eurasian Union, including countries like Ukraine, Kazakhstan and Belarus (which were part of the original Silk Road), to ensure these countries fall under Russian influence, rather than Chinese. This move is a great concern for the Chinese leaders, who fear Moscow may try to keep Beijing away from what it considers its 'zone of influence'. Finnair is in a very interesting position to expand its services into Russia and other countries in the Eurasian Union, further augmenting its potential to increase activities via a second network of Silk Road routes.[3] For Asia, Finnair has also expanded their European network, so that Asian passengers can more easily connect to other locations in Europe. This also offers the opportunity of promoting tourism in Finland, as transit passengers might be lured to visit some parts of Finland during a short stopover. For that reason, Finnair increased frequencies on its domestic network. The airline even signed a strategic partnership with a major Chinese travel platform, making Helsinki one of their key European gateways to destinations in Finnish Lapland and Europe. At the same time, Finnair augmented its presence on Chinese social media with messages and movies, promoting tourism to Finland in Chinese languages.[4] Furthermore, Chinese passengers can book tickets on Chinese websites like Quanar.com and Ctrip. About 36.4 per cent of Chinese travellers prefer to book their tickets via these websites, rather than booking a flight via the official website of the airline.[5]

In 2017, Finnair once again increased its workforce by more than one thousand people.[6] By the end of the year, the airline opened its new COOL Nordic Cargo terminal, which is partly using own solar power. In October, Finnair announced that it would acquire 60 per cent of Norra from Staffpoint Holding Oy and Kilco Oy. Finnair owned 40 per cent of the company prior to the transaction. In November, Norra transferred to the full ownership of Finnair on an interim basis, while Finnair was looking for a new industrial partner to further develop Norra's business with Finnair. Finally, Finnair would sell 60 per cent of the shares to Danish Air Transport. As a result of its growth, the airline could end the year with an operational profit of €170m (£144.6m).[7] The airline had added new routes to Goa (India), Havana (Cuba), Puerto Plata (Dominican Republic), Puerto Vallarta (Mexico), San Francisco and Reykjavik and added more frequency to popular destinations like Hong Kong (from seven flights per week to ten flights per week), Bangkok (from 14 flights per week to 16 flights), Singapore (from five flights to seven flights per week) and Tokyo. It was decided to start up a new route to Nanjing, the seventh destination in Greater China. By the end of the year, Finnair had transported almost 12 million passengers, and, during the summer of 2017, the airline reached a new record when the number of daily passengers increased to over 40,000. Notwithstanding expanding frequencies and destinations, Finnair reduced its carbon dioxide emissions per available tonne kilometre by as much as 6.7 per cent, in part due to the introduction of new aircraft. When asked about fleet development, Finnair denied it had plans to switch some of its A350-900 orders into the larger -1000 variant. The Finnish carrier was the launch customer for the A350-900, whereas Qatar Airways had been the launch-customer for the A350-1000.[8] In the meantime, Finnair's last A340 had made its last flight from Narita in Tokyo to Helsinki on 31 January 2017.[9]

For the third consecutive year in a row, Finnair experienced a rapid growth in 2018 with a full-year traffic growth of 14.8 per cent (and a capacity increase by 11.6 per cent). Capacity was added mainly on Asian routes, while Nanjing was added to the route network. In the second part of the year, capacity on European routes was also increased. The fleet of ATR aircraft, used on domestic flights in Finland, but also on regional flights to the Baltic states, Gdańsk in Poland and Stockholm Bromma Airport, would receive a renewed cabin. These aircraft are operated by Finnair's partner Norra on a contract flying basis. The cabin renewal of the 12 aircraft would start in 2019 and had to be completed in the first quarter of 2020. In the meantime, a new Nordic Business Class concept was introduced, which enables a more personal service that caters to the individual needs of passengers. To further extend its Scandinavian footprint, Finnair signed a cooperation agreement with Norway-based Widerøe. Widerøe is Northern Europe's largest regional carrier, and thanks to codeshare agreements, Finnair could add several new routes to its flight schedule. Widerøe would also operate Finnair's flights from Helsinki to Bergen and Tromso on Finnair's behalf.[10]

For Topi Manner, the new president and CEO of the airline, the first year in office was, however, not without problems. Extreme weather conditions – harsh winters, typhoons in Asia and an exceptionally warm summer in Finland – impacted Finnair's traffic, punctuality and demand. The excellent summer weather delayed bookings and weakened demand for package tours to popular sunny destinations in the Mediterranean. In the third quarter, domestic and short-haul traffic were adversely affected by runway work at Helsinki-Vantaa and Tampere airports. Notwithstanding these problems, the airline managed to increase its passenger load factor to 81.8 per cent.

Finnair agreed with Airbus to accelerate delivery of two A350s. Originally planned to be delivered in 2022 and 2023, delivery would now take place in 2019 and 2020. As Finnair had decided to keep the A330s in service, it was decided cabins would be renewed in 2020–22.[11] Thanks to an enlarged fleet of long-haul aircraft, Finnair could also plan the start-up of a new route to Los Angeles with A350 equipment. The airline would start to fly three frequencies to Los Angeles per week as of 31 March 2019. The new route to the US would be the first route to North America operated with the new A350. Routes to San Francisco and Chicago were added again to the summer schedule with four frequencies to San Francisco. This way, Finnair would offer daily connections between Northern Europe and California. The new routes would be operated within the Atlantic joint business between Finnair, American Airlines, British Airways and Iberia.[12] Of course, destinations in China would remain the core of Finnair's operations. In an interview with *China Daily*, Pekka Vauramo (then Finnair's president and CEO) commented on Chinese tourists visiting Rovaniemi in Finland. 'One could think the hometown of Santa Claus would only be busy once a year – but it's humming all year round thanks to the influx of Chinese travellers', he stated.[13] 'People need a reason to travel and Finnair is eager to offer them that reason', he said. At the time of the interview, Vauramo was in Beijing to celebrate the 30th anniversary of Finnair's Helsinki–Beijing nonstop service, which started in June 1988. Since that moment, the airline had carried more than 2.65 million passengers between both cities. In 2018, Finnair topped all European airlines in providing 38 weekly flights to seven destinations in China (Beijing, Shanghai, Chongqing, Xi'an, Nanjing, Guangzhou and Hong Kong). To facilitate tax-free purchases by Chinese clients, Finnair was the first airline worldwide to launch the Alipay online payment service on long-haul flights to China in 2017 and has doubled its onboard duty-free goods sales since.

Finnair introduced the Nordic Business Class lounge at Helsinki-Vantaa Airport. (Finnair)

A Nordic Business Class seat aboard Finnair's new aircraft. (Finnair)

Above left: A traditional salmon dish, served aboard the A350 in business class. (Finnair)

Above right: Part of the Finnair fleet at Helsinki-Vantaa airport. (Finavia)

Above: Finnair accelerated delivery of two Airbus A350s. (N509FZ/Wikimedia Commons Licence)

Right: Flight preparations for a Finnair flight. (Finnair)

Chapter 14
COVID-19

By all standards, 2019 was once again a very successful year for Finnair, even if it was a volatile period. With a capacity growth of 11.3 per cent in passenger volume and an increase of 10.3 per cent in passenger numbers, the airline obtained an income growth of 9.2 per cent. At the end of the year, the airline could publish a profit of €162.8m (£138.6m). Volatility in the sector was mainly created by the continuing impact of global uncertainty relating to the Brexit and the US–China trade war. This reflected in Finnair's operations in 2019, especially affecting cargo. Traffic grew at a slower pace than in previous years. On the other hand, competitors' reductions on some Nordic routes from Finland to the Mediterranean had a beneficial effect on Finnair's activities. In intra-European traffic from Finland, Finnair's market shares even increased to 60 per cent.[1]

Once again, routes to the Far East contributed to the growth of the airline. Finnair had started up flights to the new Beijing Daxing International Airport, as well as to Sapporo in Japan, while frequencies on other routes had again been increased. Finnair also announced it would introduce flights to Busan, the second largest city in South Korea in the summer of 2020. A little later, the airline would also start up flights to Tokyo Haneda, which offers a faster connection to central Tokyo than Narita International Airport. To further strengthen Finnair's position in China, the airline launched a codeshare cooperation with China Southern, the largest carrier in China with a fleet of over 800 aircraft. The cooperation included the Finnair route between Guangzhou and Helsinki, and selected China Southern destinations in China. This way, customers would be able to connect with China Southern from Guangzhou to Changsha, Chongqing, Hangzhou, Nanjing, Sanya, Wenzhou, Xiamen and Xi'an. In exchange, China Southern's code would be added to Finnair flights from Helsinki to several popular destinations in Europe.[2] In order to be able to further increase Asian business, Finnair planned to invest up to €4bn (£3.4bn) in new aircraft between 2020 and 2025. This would increase the fleet from 83 aircraft to approximately 100 aircraft. This fleet expansion would include both narrow-body and wide-body aircraft, resulting in a fleet ratio of 70 per cent narrow-body and 30 per cent wide-body aircraft by 2025. Some of the narrow-body aircraft might also be used on longer trips. With the new Airbus A321LR, Finnair would like to start up flights from Helsinki to China's so-called second cities, where passenger demand does not warrant the use of wide-bodies.

Other highlights for 2019 were the renewal of the ATR aircraft cabins, the opening of a new Platinum Wing lounge in the Helsinki-Vantaa Airport, and the installation of wireless internet access on Airbus narrow-body aircraft. In August 2019, Finnair also operated its first 'Push for Change' biofuel flight from San Francisco to Helsinki. This service offers passengers the possibility of offsetting the CO_2 emissions of their flights through an emission reduction project and/or through the support of the use of biofuel on Finnair flights. That year also saw Finnair proudly celebrate 50 years of service to the United States.

A year later, enthusiasm turned into disaster. The year 2020 will go down in history as the most difficult peacetime year in commercial aviation's 100 years of existence. The COVID-19 pandemic has been first and foremost a human crisis and a health crisis, which has touched hundreds of millions of people globally, whose livelihoods depend on international travel, including Finnair. Amid lockdowns and exceptional restrictions to travel across countries and continents, airlines suffered massive losses as passenger flows diminished or disappeared completely. During the year, Finnair carried 3.5 million passengers, 14.7 per cent of the normal annual passenger number.

Revenues shrank to €829m (£706m), compared to €3,097m (£2,640m) a year earlier. As a result, the airline made a loss of €595m (£507m). In the spring of 2020, the airline operated with a capacity of a few per cent only, maintaining critical connections for Finland to key European cities. Even if people did not travel, goods had to keep moving, and the airline quickly ramped up its cargo-only operations. With increased demand for the transportation of health-related products, the airline had decided, for the time being, to convert some of its passenger aircraft into cargo aircraft by removing the seats. All in all, the airline operated 1,300 cargo flights during 2020, and cargo – supported by the shortage of capacity and increased prices in the market – played a significant role in the revenue. In the summer of 2020, Finnair started increasing the number of passenger flights, but the pandemic situation continued to be challenging, and Finnair operated only a limited network of approximately 50 destinations and 75 daily flights throughout the rest of the year. The airline had to pay €460m (£391.7m) in refunds for cancelled flights.

In order to survive, Finnair raised approximately €1.8bn (£1.53bn) of new financing, including an oversubscribed rights issue of over €500m (£426m). Finnair became the first European airline to sell a bond since the coronavirus pandemic began, paying a double-digit rate of interest to raise higher-risk debt with equity-like features. The debt has a perpetual maturity, meaning that it never has to be repaid, but guarantees a 10.25 per cent annual interest rate.[3] The airline could also borrow €600m (£511m) from its pension fund. In addition, together with the State of Finland, the airline prepared a hybrid loan of up to €400m (£341m), which had to be approved by the EU Commission. In the beginning of 2021, the European Commission agreed that Finnish government support to the amount of €351m (£299m) was in line with EU state aid rules.[4] To reduce costs, almost all personnel were furloughed for at least a part of the year. About 1,100 people lost their jobs permanently. Delivery of three Airbus A350s, scheduled for the second quarter of 2021 and 2022, was postponed. Based on the new agreement, the remaining three aircraft will be delivered in 2022, 2024 and 2025. At the same time, Finnair also retired two of its oldest A319 aircraft.

To restore customers' trust in air travel, the airline introduced several health measures, such as intensified aircraft cleaning, plastic screens at the airport customer service points, minimisation of unnecessary human contact on board, new boarding and disembarkation processes, and more. Finnair also offered a complimentary Corona Cover, extending customers' own travel insurance to all international flights departing from Finland. The insurance compensates, to a great deal, potential COVID-19 related costs accrued during a trip. Obviously, the traditional Santa Claus flights were cancelled. Instead, Finnair operated eight virtual flights from Helsinki to Rovaniemi to meet Santa. The total proceeds of these virtual flights – about €90,000 (£76,600) – went to supporting UNICEF's work to slow the spread of COVID-19 and minimise the pandemic's impact on children worldwide.

Of course, the pandemic was not gone in 2021. Travel restrictions had been lifted at a slower pace than expected, and therefore the recovery in demand was also delayed. Finnair once again operated a limited network, adding flights as demand evolved when European countries started to open for travel. The route to New York re-opened in the spring, and routes to Chicago and Los Angeles were also re-introduced. In the entire passenger network, Finnair carried 600,000 passengers during the first half of the year. Cargo demand, however, remained strong because of the delivery chain challenges caused by the pandemic. In the first half of 2021, Finnair flew 522 cargo-only flights, which accounted for more than half of its revenues. As a result, the airline had to book an operating loss of €288m (£245m). In order to raise funds, Finnair was selling and leasing back four of its A350 aircraft. The transaction, involving four aircraft that were delivered between June 2017 and February 2019, freed up cash of over €200m (£170.4m). The airline will use the funds to refinance existing debt. The counterparts of the transaction were lessors GECAS and PIMCO.[5,6]

While Finnair was keeping its balance sheet in equilibrium, the airline was also taking steps to grow, once the pandemic was over. As Asia would remain the major destination of its flights, the airline signed a joint business partnership with Juneyao Air on the Helsinki–Shanghai route. The two airlines had started a codeshare operation in July 2019, when Juneyao Air launched its Shanghai to Helsinki route. The joint business partnership deepened the partnership, providing corporate and leisure customers with more flexible routing options, attractive fares and enhanced benefits for frequent flyer members. Finnair customers would benefit from improved connectivity to a network of 57 destinations in China from Juneyao's Shanghai hub, and Juneyao customers would enjoy better access to Finnair's extensive network of 65 European destinations via its Helsinki hub.[7]

As is often the case, the problems of one airline might become the advantage of another carrier. Finnair might indeed be one of the few airlines that could see its home market expand when the pandemic recedes. The carrier's Nordic competition is receding, leaving it in a good place to swoop in and grab market shares when travel resumes. Finnair's main competitor in the region, Norwegian Air, had to scale back its operations. As part of the restructuring plan it hammered out with its home government, Norwegian reduced its fleet from 140 aircraft to just 50 aircraft, all narrow bodies. The airline also gave up its intercontinental ambitions. Finnair's rival SAS, based in Oslo and Copenhagen, was also scaling back its Helsinki base. According to Finnair, this situation would leave about 3 million passengers up for grabs in the Finnish market. The bankruptcy of the HNA Group and its airlines' downsizing could create more opportunities for Finnair in the Chinese market, but one can imagine Chinese carriers will more quickly step in to fill any absence left by HNA.[8]

Finnair, which was established nearly a century ago, managed to overcome major problems, unlike many of other carriers. World War Two, the banking crisis, natural disasters and downturns of the economy did not stop Finnair's growth. Thanks to its very strong Asian connection, the airline is successfully operating in a very specific growth market, which will only further expand in the near future. The COVID-19 crisis is, of course, a major problem for the Finnish carrier, like it is for all other airlines in the world. However, Finnair, while fighting back to survive, is already taking steps for the post-COVID period, in which it once again wants to excel as a modern premium airline linking Europe and Asia.

In 2019, Finnair celebrated 50 years of flying to the United States. (Finnair)

Also in 2019, Finnair renewed the cabins of its ATR fleet. (Finnair)

The ATR fleet made it possible to build an extensive network of Scandinavian routes. (Finnair)

When the COVID-19 pandemic hit the world, Finnair converted its A330s from passenger aircraft to cargo aircraft. (Finnair)

Of course, Finnair follows strict COVID-19 protocols. (Finnair)

Accidents and Incidents

(Based upon information from the Accident Safety Network)

On 16 November 1927, an Aero Oy Junkers F 13 disappeared en route from Tallinn to Helsinki. The aircraft was carrying two Finnish officers and the pilot. The pilot probably got lost, landed on water and the plane sank.

On 10 November 1937, an Aero Oy Junkers Ju 52's nose engine dropped off into the sea during a scheduled flight from Turku to Stockholm. The pilots managed to land safely with the two remaining engines. A broken propeller blade had caused a severe imbalance, tearing the engine off its mounting.

On 14 June 1940, an Aero Oy Junkers Ju 52/3 aircraft flying from Tallinn to Helsinki was shot down by two Soviet SB-2 bombers over the Gulf of Finland. At that time, there was no war between the Soviet Union and Finland. Among the passengers were the French diplomatic couriers, Paul Longuet and Frederic Marty, and the American courier, Henry Antheil, from the American embassy in Helsinki. The Soviet Union had declared an embargo on Estonia on 9 June 1940, and the Soviet air force was ordered to prevent Estonian and Latvian air force flights to Finland or Sweden. Various theories for the shootdown have been presented, one being that the Soviet Union wanted to get hold of the diplomatic mail that was transported in the aircraft. According to an article in *Yle Uutiset*, published on 4 August 2008, an American military probe had failed to find the wreckage of the aircraft. The six-day search operation had been operated by a US Navy oceanographic survey ship. Prior to this search, Estonia had asked for American help in trying to locate the wreck. Therefore, theories stating the wreck was picked up by a Soviet submarine that was operating in the area at the time of the downing, become more trustworthy.

On 7 November 1941, an Aero Oy Junkers Ju 52/3 aircraft equipped with floats made an emergency landing in the sea after all three engines had failed because of problems with the quality of the fuel. The two persons on board drowned while trying to swim to safety. The aircraft was later repaired.

On 31 October 1945, an Aero Oy Junkers Ju 52/3 aircraft approached Hyvinkää in poor weather. Radio signals were distorted by high voltage overhead wires and the aircraft descended below minimum altitude and crashed in a forest. All 14 passengers on board survived, but the aircraft was written off.

On 3 January 1961, a Douglas DC-3 operating flight 311 from Kronoby to Vaasa stalled on final approach and crashed, killing all 25 people on board. According to the investigators, the probable cause of the accident was the wrong execution of a left turn at low altitude at night, which caused the aircraft to stall, lose its manoeuvrability and go into a spin. As a consequence of alcoholic intoxication and insufficient sleep the night before, the pilot was not considered to be in the satisfactory mental and physical condition to undertake the flight. For the same reason, the co-pilot should not have been allowed to start the flight in question. The accident remains the deadliest accident in Finnish aviation history.

On 8 November 1963, an Aero Oy Douglas DC-3 operating flight 217 on route from Helsinki via Turku to Mariehamn crashed during a non-precision approach to Mariehamn in the Åland Islands. Of the 25 people on board, only three survived. During the approach, the aircraft had struck trees in a nearly horizontal attitude before the threshold of the runway. The plane flipped over and caught fire. Before the accident, ILS (Instrument Landing System) equipment had been ordered for the airport, but local land use disputes had prevented an installation. The investigation board considered that the ultimate cause of the accident was the pilot's misconception of his altitude. A defect was found in the pilot-in-command's altimeter. It is also clear the flight had left Turku in violation of regulations regarding poor visibility at the destination. These conditions were worse than the weather approved for runway 20 in Mariehamn.

On 30 September 1978, Finnair flight 405 from Oulu to Helsinki, flown by a Sud Aviation Caravelle, was hijacked by Aarno Lamminparras, who was armed with a pistol. At that time, Finland did not perform security checks on domestic flights. The hijacker held the 48 passengers and crew hostage. The aircraft continued to Helsinki, where 34 of the 44 passengers were released before the aircraft returned to Oulu, where the hijacker received a large ransom from Finnair. The plane then returned to Helsinki for another ransom from a Finnish newspaper, before flying to Amsterdam and then back to Oulu via Helsinki. The hijacker released the last hostages and departed the aircraft before being arrested at his home on 1 October.

On 23 December 1987, Finnair flight 915 from Tokyo to Helsinki was allegedly shot at by a missile whilst over Svalbard (Spitsbergen). The missile allegedly exploded in the air before striking the Douglas DC-10. It is very strange that the incident, revealed by the newspaper *Helsingin Sanomat*, had come to light only in 2014, because, according to the crew members, the aircraft's captain refused to submit a report. According to the article, a missile appeared in the distance when the aircraft was crossing the Arctic Ocean, two hours from its destination. The crew thought it was a Russian weather rocket on its way into space, but the missile then slowed down, turned, and began heading straight towards the aircraft. Moments later, just 20 seconds away from a collision, the missile exploded. Despite the potential for a large-scale loss of life, a serious incident report was not written. The co-pilots claim they informed the captain, who was resting and therefore not in the cockpit at the time of the incident, but he never reported the incident. Finnair's records contain no mention of the dramatic near miss. According to *Yle Uutiset* (9 September 2014), the question of who fired the missile has never been definitively answered. The pilots believed it was launched from either the Soviet Union's Kola Peninsula or a submarine in the Barents Sea. The pair also said they did not believe Soviet forces deliberately wanted to shoot down the aircraft, and think the missile was either fired in error or that the aircraft was used as a training target. According to *Helsingin Sanomat*, the Finnish government was only informed about the incident 27 years later, when the article about the mishap was published in the newspapers. If the origin of the missile remains a mystery, it also remains a mystery why the crew did not file a detailed report about the incident.[1]

Fleet Details

Finnair Historical Fleet Details

(Source: Finnair)

Aircraft Type	Number Used	First Introduction in Fleet	Removed from Active Fleet
DOUGLAS DC-8-60/70	4	1969	1984
McDONNELL DOUGLAS DC-9-10	9	1971	1988
McDONNELL DOUGLAS DC-9-50	12	1976	2003
McDONNELL DOUGLAS DC-10-30	5	1981	1996
McDONNELL DOUGLAS DC-9-40	5	1981	1995
McDONNELL DOUGLAS MD-83	13	1985	2006
ATR 42	6	1986	1990
McDONNELL DOUGLAS MD-87	3	1987	2000
BOEING 737-200C	2	1989	1993
AIRBUS A300-B4	2	1990	1998
McDONNELL DOUGLAS MD-11F	7	1991	2011
McDONNELL DOUGLAS MD-82	10	1993	2006
ATR 72	9	1995	2005
SAAB 340	7	1996	2000
BOEING 757-200	7	1992	2014
AIRBUS A319-100	5	1999	2020
AIRBUS A320-200	2	2002	2012
EMBRAER ERJ-170	10	2005	2016
AIRBUS A340-300	7	2006	2017

Finnair Current Fleet Details

(Source: Finnair)

(Not all these aircraft are currently in service. The number of parked aircraft changes from week to week, depending upon the evolution of the COVID-19 pandemic)

Aircraft Type	Delivered	On Order
AIRBUS A350 XWB	16	3
AIRBUS A330-300	8	
AIRBUS A321	19	
AIRBUS A320	10	
AIRBUS A319	6	
EMBRAER 190	12	
ATR 72 (operated by Norra)	12	

Notes and References

Chapter 1

1. 'The Growth of Finnish Civil Aviation and the Finnish Aviation Industry through the 1920's and 1930's', *Alternative Finland*, March 2017
2. 'Finnair's Maiden Flight 90 years ago was all-German', *Yle Uutiset*, 19 March 2014
3. 'The Growth of Finnish Civil Aviation and the Finnish Aviation Industry through the 1920's and 1930's', *Alternative Finland*, March 2017
4. ibid
5. 'The Early Years of Finland's Air Travel and the Construction of Civil Airports', *Alternative Finland*, April 2017
6. National Union of Students, 'Finland – the Outpost of the North', November 1937

Chapter 2

1. 'Winter War', en.wikipedia.org
2. 'Continuation War', en.wikipedia.org

Chapter 3

1. 'Finnair', en.wikipedia.org
2. Pallini, Thomas, 'Finnair Celebrates 50 years of service to New York', AirlineGeeks.com, 9 June 2019

Chapter 4

1. 'Finnair', fi.wikimedia.org
2. 'Finnair', en.wikipedia.org
3. ibid

Chapter 5

1. 'Karair', en.wikipedia.org
2. 'Alcazar', en.wikipedia.org
3. 'Finnair', en.wikipedia.org
4. ibid
5. 'Finncomm airlines', en.wikipedia.org
6. 'Finncomm has started in-service training for its pilots', Svenska.Yle.fi, 18 February 2007
7. 'Finnair PLC has signed a preliminary agreement on a corporate transaction with Finncomm OY', Finnair Company Announcement, 9 September 2010
8. 'Finncomm Group has sold Finnish Commuter Airlines to a Flybe & Finnair joint venture', Oaklins Finland Corporate Information
9. 'Nordic Regional Airlines', Wikiwand

Chapter 6

1. *Finnair Annual Report 1998*, Report by the Chief Executive Officer, Finnair, January 1999
2. ibid
3. ibid
4. 'Cooperation around the World', *Finnair Annual Report 1999*, Finnair, January 2000

Chapter 7

1. 'Changes in operating environment support Finnair's Nordic role', *Finnair Annual Report 1999*, Finnair, February 2000.
2. 'Aero Airlines', en.wikipedia.org
3. 'Salient Events in the financial year', *Finnair Annual Report 2001*, Finnair, February 2002
4. ibid

Chapter 8

1. 'Difficulties in the past and ahead', *Finnair Annual Report 2002*, Finnair, February 2003
2. 'Flying Finn', fi.wikipedia.org
3. 'Flying Finn', en.wikipedia.org
4. 'Nordic Airlink', en.wikipedia.org
5. *Finnair Annual Report 2002*, Finnair, February 2003
6. *Finnair Annual Report 2005*, Finnair, January 2006

Chapter 9

1. *Finnair Annual Report 2006*, Finnair, February 2007
2. ibid
3. Jokivuori, Pertti Juhani, 'Strike at Finnair over restructuring is settled by conciliation', Eurofound, eurofound.europa.eu, 12 December 2006
4. Jokivuori, Pertti Juhani, 'Restructuring Dispute at Finnair continues', Eurofound, eurofound.europa.eu, 21 December 2008
5. Jokivuori, Pertii Juhani, 'Impartiality of national conciliator in Finnair dispute questioned', Eurofound, eurofound.europa.eu, 13 April 2009
6. *IATA Annual Report 2009*, IATA, January 2010
7. ibid
8. ibid
9. ibid
10. *Finnair Annual Report 2009*, Finnair, February 2010
11. Jokivuori, Pertti Juhani,'Former national conciliator called to resolve airport outsourcing dispute', Eurofound, eurofound.europa.eu, 16 February 2010

Chapter 10

1. 'Finnair's last MD-11 passenger flight', *Airline World*, 23 February 2010
2. 'Paper to Mug – Long live the Moomins', Finnair, 1996
3. Maslen, Richard, 'And finally – Finnair's Angry Birds flight to Singapore', routesonline.com, 22 September 2011
4. *IATA Annual Report 2010*, February 2011
5. ibid
6. *Finnair Annual Report 2010*, Finnair, January 2011

7. *IATA Annual Report 2010*, February 2011
8. *IATA Annual Report 2011*, January 2012
9. *Finnair Annual Report 2010*, Finnair, January 2011

Chapter 11

1. *IATA Annual Report 2010*, February 2011
2. *IATA Annual Report 2011*, January 2012
3. 'Finnair in 2011', *Finnair Financial Report 2011*, February 2012
4. Jokivuori, Pertti, 'Finnair strike injunction criticised by unions and legal experts', Eurofound, eurofound.europa.eu, 24 July 2012
5. *Finnair Annual Report 2012*, Finnair, February 2013
6. 'Finnair', en.wikipedia.org
7. Mann, Rebecca, 'Finnair and Marimekko launch inflight design collaboration', *The Moodie Report*, 8 November 2012
8. Paakkanen, Mikko, 'Finnair and Marimekko seek growth in China', *Helsinki Times*, 24 October 2014
9. *Finnair Annual Report 2013*, Finnair, January 2014

Chapter 12

1. *Finnair Annual Report 2014*, Finnair, January 2015
2. ibid
3. 'Finnair firms up orders for eight additional A350 aircraft', Finnair Media Desk, 3 December 2014
4. Orban, André, 'Finnair signs memorandum of understanding on the sale and leaseback of three Embraer 190 aircraft', Aviation24.be, 17 December 2014
5. *Finnair Group Financial Statements Bulletin 2015*, Finnair, January 2016
6. Persson, Joakim, 'First in Europe with the next-gen aircraft Finnair debuts Airbus A350 XWB to Shanghai', Scandasia.com, 11 October 2015
7. 'Finnair adds seating capacity to its feeder fleet', Finnair, Stock Exchange Release, 18 December 2015
8. 'Airberlin's A321 aircraft arrived to fly Finnair's European flights', Lentoposti, 1 May 2015
9. Finnair Group Financial Statements Bulletin 2015, Finnair, January 2016

Chapter 13

1. *Finnair Annual Report 2016*, Finnair, January 2017.
2. Bruce-Lockhart, Anna, 'The new Silk Road', World Economic Forum, 26 June 2017
3. Brugier, Camille, 'China's way: the new Silk Road', European Union Institute for Security Studies, www.iss.europa.eu, May 2014
4. Wei, Sheng, *Brand image of Finnair among young wealthy Chinese in Chinese social media*, thesis, Lapland University of Applied Sciences, 2015
5. ibid
6. *Finnair Annual Report 2017*, Finnair, January 2018.
7. ibid
8. Hofmann, Kurt, 'Finnair denies interest in A350-1000; expands long-haul network', *ATW Air Transport World*, 18 January 2017
9. 'The last flight of a four-engine Airbus A340 in Finnair's colors is over', Lentoposti.fi, 1 February 2017

10. 'Finnair extends its network in Norway by deepening cooperation with Wideroe', *Finnair News*, 15 May 2018
11. 'Finnair's growth continues – the narrow-body project is progressing', Lentoposti.fi, 25 April 2018
12. 'Finnair to fly new A350 route to Los Angeles in 2019', *Finnair News*, 21 August 2018
13. Tao Hu, 'Finnair flying high with China's ongoing growth and development', *China Daily*, 15 June 2018

Chapter 14

1. *Finnair Annual Report 2019*, Finnair, February 2020
2. 'Finnair and China Southern launch codeshare cooperation that brings five new destinations for Finnair customers in China', *Finnair News*, 21 May 2019
3. Asgari, Nikou, 'Finnair in first bond sale by European airline since pandemic began', *Financial Times*, 27 August 2020
4. Orban, André, 'European commission approves around 350m euro Finnish support to compensate Finnair for damages suffered due to coronavirus outbreak', Aviation24.be, March 16, 2021
5. 'Finnair uses A350s to raise cash in sale and leaseback deal', Aerotime.aero, 28 September 2021
6. Orban, André, 'Finnair signs sale and leaseback agreement for four A350 aircraft for refinancing in excess of 400 million USD', Aviation24.be, 28 September 2021
7. 'Finnair and Juneyao Air enter into a joint business partnership on the Helsinki-Shanghai route and beyond', *Finnair News*, 23 June 2021
8. Unnikrishnan, Madhu, 'Finnair sees opportunity in Norwegian's woes', *Airline Weekly*, 22 February 2021

Appendix 1

1. 'HS: Finnair pilots report dramatic missile near-miss almost 30 years on', *Yle Uutiset*, 7 September 2018